The Family Finance Playbook

Essential Strategies For Building Financial Literacy Together

By

Jeff Kikel, ChFC, CRPC, CCFS

MEDIA LLC

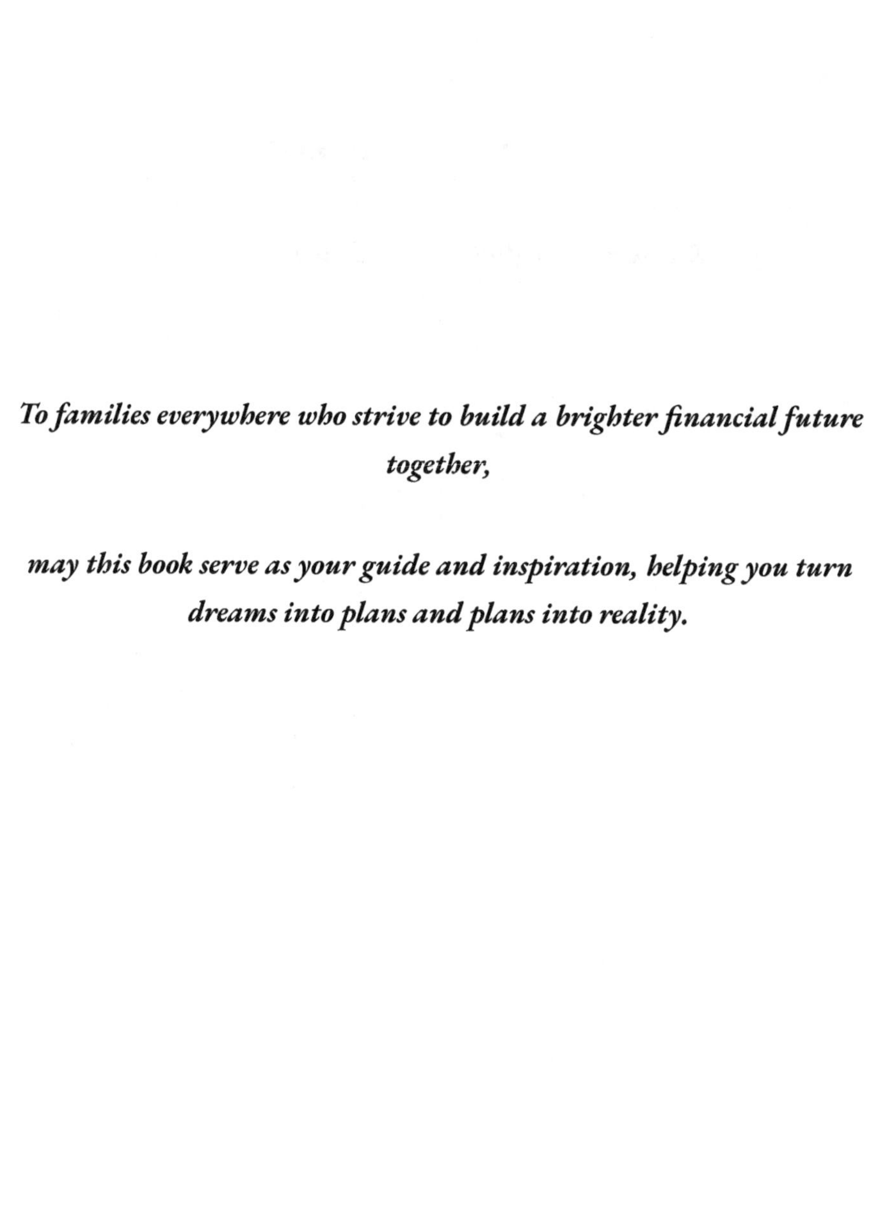

To families everywhere who strive to build a brighter financial future together,

may this book serve as your guide and inspiration, helping you turn dreams into plans and plans into reality.

Legal Disclaimer

This book, "Family Finance Playbook," is intended for informational and educational purposes only. It does not provide specific financial, legal, or tax advice. While the author is a registered investment advisor, the content of this book is not intended as individual investment advice or as a recommendation for specific investment actions.

The strategies, tips, and tools described in this book are provided as general guidance for personal finance management. They are not specific advice tailored to the individual circumstances of their readers. The scenarios and examples provided in this book are hypothetical and included for illustrative purposes only. They are not guarantees of future performance or success and should not be taken as precise financial guidance.

Readers should consult professional financial advisors, lawyers, or other competent experts before making serious financial decisions. The author specifically disclaims any liability, loss, or risk, personal or otherwise, which is incurred as a consequence, directly or indirectly, of the use and application of any of the contents of this book.

This book does not replace the need for professional advice tailored to your individual circumstances. The information provided herein is accurate as of the date of publication and is subject to change based on market and other conditions.

Using this book, you agree that the author is not responsible for the success or failure of your financial decisions relating to any information presented.

Books by Jeff Kikel

Gen X and Late Boomer Series

The Retirement Income Equation: Proven Strategies for a Secure, Flexible, and Prosperous Retirement

7 Critical Mistakes To Avoid In Retirement Planning: A Comprehensive Guide To Avoiding Common Pitfalls And Securing Your Financial Future

Freedom Day Series

Overcoming The Retirement Trap: An 8-Step Financial Freedom Blueprint For Your Journey To Building Wealth, Creating Financial Independence, and A Life Beyond Limits

The Get The Nerve™ Series with Joe Serio, PhD

Leaving Blue: 50 Lessons On Retiring Well From Law Enforcement

With Gary Kasper

Identity Theft: The Road To Recovery

Contents

Forward

Hey there! Ever feel like the world of money is a secret club that no one taught you the handshake for? You're not alone. It seems like everywhere we turn, some new financial term or investment trend is popping up, making us wonder, "Should I know about this?" The truth is, many folks are in the same boat, cruising through life without a financial compass. And guess what? It's not entirely our fault.

At home, money talk is often as rare as a unicorn sighting. "How much do we save? Why is credit important?" These questions could be spoken in an ancient language for all the attention they get. And at school? Forget about it. For some reason, figuring out the angle of a triangle is deemed more crucial than learning how to budget or save for the future. Go figure.

Introducing your new financial allies, the *Family Financial Playbook,* and our TV show, *Your Family Your Finances* on Your Home TV network (www.yourhometv.com). These resources are not just another set of financial guides. They are your personal financial mentors, designed to illuminate the world of finances for families everywhere, and help you all speak the same money language.

Get ready to unlock the secrets of money matters. The *Family Financial Playbook* and the *Your Family Your Finances* show differ from your typical financial guides. They are your golden tickets to a world of financial understanding, presented in a fun, relatable, and most importantly, helpful way. We're not here to lecture. We're here to guide you through the jungle of finances with a machete of knowledge, cutting down the myths and mysteries that have kept us in the dark for too long.

Imagine the thrill of discussing savings, investments, and budgeting as easily as you talk about your favorite Netflix series or the latest game drop. That's the power of the *Family*

Financial Playbook and *Your Family Your Finances* TV shows. They're not just about financial literacy; they're about empowerment.

We want you to feel informed, inspired, and ready to confidently take on your financial future. And hey, we promise to keep it as entertaining as discovering a new favorite playlist.

So, whether you're sixteen or sixty, it's always early enough to get savvy about your finances. Let's kickstart those dinner table conversations about money, swap fear for fun when it comes to budgeting, and turn financial planning into a family adventure. Together, we will build a solid foundation to support, not just your dreams, but those of future generations.

Welcome to your family's financial awakening. Let's make it awesome.

—Jeff Kikel

May 2024 - Cedar Park, TX

Introduction

In today's fast-paced world, where financial landscapes are continually evolving, the need for comprehensive financial literacy has never been more critical. The *Family Finance Playbook* is a guide and a companion on your journey to transforming your family's financial future. We're here with you every step of the way, aiming to demystify the world of finances for you and your older children.

Purpose of the Playbook

This playbook has a dual mission: to enhance your understanding of essential financial concepts and equip your family with the tools needed for financial success. It's about laying a solid foundation, not just for today, but for generations to come. We blend timeless financial principles with modern strategies to create a robust framework for managing, saving, and investing money, ensuring your family's secure and prosperous future.

What You Will Gain

- **Empowerment:** Learn to navigate the financial world confidently, making informed decisions that align with your family's goals and values.

- **Engagement:** Through interactive activities, discussions, and practical exercises, we turn financial learning into a shared family adventure. Get ready to dive in, ask questions, and learn together in a fun and engaging way.

- **Education:** Dive deep into budgeting, saving, investing, and much more with clear, actionable guidance tailored for parents and older children.

As we explore the realms of financial literacy together, remember that this playbook is just the beginning. We encourage you to visit YourFamilyYourFinances.com for additional resources, updates, and in-depth information. Furthermore, to bring these concepts to life, watch the latest episodes of *Your Family Your Finances* on yfyf.YourHomeTV.com, where we tackle these topics in a dynamic, engaging format.

Whether you're looking to break free from the cycle of living paycheck to paycheck, save for your child's education, or build lasting wealth, the *Family Finance Playbook* is your companion. Together, let's unlock the doors to financial literacy and set the stage for a future filled with possibilities.

Chapter 1

Building A Financial Foundation Together

"Financial peace isn't the acquisition of stuff. It's learning to live on less than you make so you can give money back and have money to invest. You can't win until you do this." - Dave Ramsey

Welcome to the journey of building your family's financial foundation. Consider this chapter the blueprint for constructing a house, where understanding money is akin to laying down the very first brick. Let's dive in, shall we?

Understanding Money

Imagine we're back in time, trading sheep for grains. Pretty inconvenient, right? That's where money comes in—a tool that replaced bartering, making exchanges easier. But money isn't just paper or metal. It's trust that has become tangible. Every coin and note signifies a promise, an agreement within society. It's fascinating when you think about it!

Money Through The Ages: A Quick Peek

- **Barter System:** Trading goods without money. Imagine swapping your video game with a friend for their skateboard. Simple, but limited.

- **Coins and Notes:** Metals were shaped into coins, representing value. Paper money came next, easier to carry and use.

- **Digital Age:** Today, money often moves as numbers on screens. Digital transactions, online shopping, and even cryptocurrencies are the norm.

Why Money Matters

Money buys us food, shelter, and education in our daily lives. It also brings joy, like vacations or that new gadget. But beyond purchases, money is about choices and freedom. Managing it well lets us live the lives we dream of, helping us support our loved ones and reach our goals.

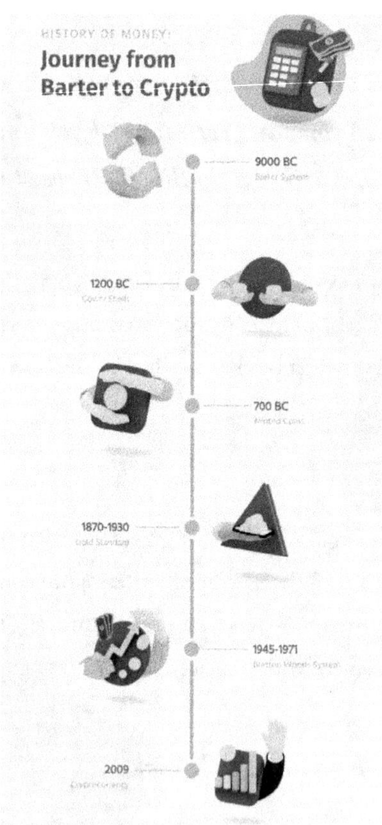

Activity: Family Money Tree

Here's a fun activity to explore money's value and significance within your family.

- **Materials Needed:** Large paper or poster board, markers, and stickers.

- **Creating Your Tree:** Draw a large tree with branches. Label each branch with categories like 'Savings,' 'Necessities,' 'Education,' and 'Fun.'

- **Discussion and Decoration:** Chat about what each category means to your family. Use stickers or drawings to represent your goals or essential financial elements in each category.

- **Reflection:** Discuss how balancing different areas can lead to a healthier financial life as a well-nourished tree grows solid and stable.

This activity is more than just crafting; it's about starting meaningful conversations on money's role in your lives, highlighting priorities and dreams. Understanding money is the first step toward financial literacy. We lay the groundwork for a future where financial decisions are made confidently and clearly by exploring its evolution, discussing its impact, and engaging in family activities. Remember, every financial choice is a brick in the foundation of your family's financial house. Let's make sure it's solid!

Financial Roles In The Family

When it comes to managing finances, think of your family as a team where everyone, regardless of age, has a unique role to play. From the primary earners who bring in the income, to the savers who guard against unnecessary expenses, and even to the decision-makers who strategize on future investments or purchases, each role is pivotal.

- **Earners:** Usually, parents or guardians contribute, but sometimes older children with part-time jobs contribute, too. Their role is crucial in generating the family's income.

- **Savers:** These are those keen on reducing expenses and saving more. Children can be excellent savers, often coming up with creative ideas to cut costs.

- **Investors:** Are members who look for opportunities to grow the family's wealth, possibly through stocks, bonds, or other investments.

- **Decision-Makers:** Parents often take the lead, but involving children in some decisions can teach them valuable lessons about prioritizing and making tough choices.

- **Philanthropists:** Encourage a role dedicated to giving back, whether through donations or volunteering, instilling a sense of responsibility and compassion towards others.

Team Effort: Strength in Collaboration

The magic happens when these roles work in harmony, not in isolation. Open discussions about finances demystify the subject and strengthen family bonds. It's about creating a space where everyone feels valued and heard, from the youngest to the eldest. Here are a few tips to foster this collaborative spirit:

- **Regular Financial Meetings:** Make them a part of your family routine, where everyone can voice their thoughts and learn from each other.

- **Respect All Contributions:** Whether it's a substantial paycheck or saving a few dollars on groceries, every effort counts towards the family's financial health.

- **Learn Together:** Use financial decisions as learning moments for children, explaining the why and how to foster a deeper understanding.

Activity: Family Finance Meeting

Your family's first financial meeting is a cornerstone event. Here's how to make it engaging and productive:

- **Schedule a Time:** Choose a time when everyone can be present without distractions, such as after dinner, or a quiet weekend afternoon.

- **Set an Agenda:** Keep it simple for the first meeting. Discuss the family budget, upcoming expenses, or saving goals.

- **Roles and Responsibilities:** Introduce the idea of financial roles. Discuss who currently does what, and if there's room for more involvement or shifting of responsibilities.

- **Goal-Setting:** Together, outline a couple of financial goals. They could be as simple as saving for a new family game, or as ambitious as planning a vacation.

- **Encourage Openness:** Foster an environment where no question is too small, and no idea is too outlandish. It's about learning and growing together.

This meeting and each family member's roles are about more than just numbers and budgets; they're about instilling values, sharing dreams, and setting the stage for a financially literate family. Remember, the goal is not to achieve perfection, but to embark on a journey of financial growth together.

Creating a Financially Healthy Environment

A financially healthy environment is like a garden; it needs care, nourishment, and regular attention to thrive. Here's how you can cultivate such an environment in your family. Make financial discussions a regular part of your family life. During meals or while doing chores together, find opportunities to weave in conversations about money, savings, and financial decisions. These types of discussions should be open discussions with no judgment. There are no stupid questions or subjects. If someone in the family does not know, it's an opportunity to discuss and have everyone learn something.

You will also want to leverage everyday moments as teachable opportunities. From a grocery shopping trip to planning a family outing, there are countless ways to discuss budgeting, cost-saving strategies, and the value of money. Although this might be a repetitive task for you, it is probably the first time that one of your kids has done it. A great way to reinforce positive behavior in family finance is to celebrate financial wins together, no matter how small. Have you saved up for that family game night? Commend the collective effort and the saving strategies that made it possible. As a parent, you are a leader in your family. Children learn a lot by observation. Demonstrate prudent financial habits, and they're likely to emulate them.

Long-term Vision: Beyond the Horizon

Setting long-term financial goals is about looking beyond the immediate horizon and planning for the future. Here's how to approach this vision. You'll want to start by dreaming together. Encourage each family member to share their dreams and aspirations. How does money play a role in achieving these dreams? Identify which dreams can evolve into long-term financial goals. Be realistic and consider the family's financial capacity and timelines.

It is important to be strategic as you design your goals. Break down these long-term goals into actionable steps. Incorporate budgeting, saving, and investing strategies to pave the path towards these objectives. It's about making incremental progress, one step at a time.

As life changes, so might your goals or strategies. Hold periodic reviews to adjust your plans, ensuring they align with your family's vision. While it is important to set realistic, and sometimes stretch goals for yourselves, you also need to have some flexibility. Although I build a list of goals for each quarter, both personally and for my businesses, it is not unusual to see me adjust and adapt goals during the quarter based on changes in my life and business.

Activity: Our Family's Financial Vision Board

A vision board is a powerful tool for manifesting goals and dreams. Creating a financial vision board can be a fun and enlightening activity for the whole family:

- **Gather Supplies:** You'll need a poster board, magazines, markers, glue, and scissors. Alternatively, you can create a digital vision board using online tools.

- **Brainstorm and Search:** Have each family member consider their financial goals and dreams. Look for images in magazines or online that represent these aspirations.

- **Create and Discuss:** Work together to arrange and glue your images onto the board. As you do, discuss why each goal is important and how you can work together to achieve it.

- **Display Your Vision:** Place your family's financial vision board somewhere visible. It will serve as a daily reminder of your collective goals and your financial wellness journey together.

This activity brings your family's financial goals to life visually and strengthens your commitment to achieving them together. It says, "These are our dreams, and we can make them a reality." By setting the stage for financial wellness in your home, you're planning for a secure future and building a legacy of financial literacy and empowerment for generations to come.

Case Study: The Robinson's Allowance Adventure

The Robinson family lives in the heart of a bustling neighborhood in Houston, TX. The parents, keen on instilling financial wisdom in their twelve-year-old twins, Alex and Jordan, decided it was time for an allowance adventure. Each week, Alex and Jordan received an allowance with the understanding that they had some freedom to spend, save, or invest it, but also a gentle nudge towards saving for future wants or needs.

Alex's Journey: Planning and Patience

Alex, with eyes set on a high-quality mountain bike to explore the trails around their home, knew it was a significant investment. This bike wasn't just any purchase; it was a dream that required planning and patience. Alex decided to save a substantial portion of the weekly allowance, setting aside a tiny bit for occasional treats. Watching the savings grow was initially slow, testing Alex's patience, but the focus remained steadfast on the ultimate goal.

Throughout this journey, Alex learned the value of delayed gratification – the ability to wait and save for something truly wanted rather than spending immediately on smaller, less meaningful items. It was a lesson in setting goals, making plans, and sticking to them, even when temptations arose.

Jordan's Path: Immediate Joys and Learning Curves

On the other hand, Jordan found joy in the smaller, immediate gratifications. A comic book here, a movie outing there – these things brought happiness. However, Jordan soon realized this spending pattern left little room for bigger dreams or unexpected opportunities. There was a turning point when a sudden opportunity for a class trip came up, and Jordan found the savings lacking.

This moment was a gentle wake-up call for Jordan. It sparked a realization about the balance between enjoying the present and planning for the future. Jordan began to set aside a part of the allowance for 'big dream' goals, learning to weigh decisions more carefully and understanding the true value of money in achieving both short-term happiness and long-term aspirations.

Family Discussions: Reflecting and Growing Together

The Robinsons made it a point to discuss their allowance adventures during family dinners, reflecting on choices, celebrating successes, and brainstorming solutions to challenges. These conversations were crucial; they were not just about money but about values, priorities, and each family member's vision for their life. Alex and Jordan shared their experiences through these discussions, learned from each other, and even inspired their parents to revisit their financial habits. The family realized that financial literacy wasn't just about saving or spending but about making informed decisions that reflect one's goals, values, and circumstances.

Conclusion: A Journey of Growth

The Robinson's allowance adventure was more than a lesson in finances; it was a journey of personal growth, family bonding, and understanding the multifaceted value of money. With their differing approaches, Alex and Jordan enriched their financial literacy, learning that whether saving for a dream bike or balancing the joy of small pleasures with future aspirations, the essence lies in thoughtful decision-making and embracing the learning curve that comes with managing money.

Wrap-Up: Building a Solid Financial Foundation Together

As we wrap up this foundational chapter of our financial journey, we must recognize that what we've embarked on is much more than a series of lessons; it's the beginning of a lifelong adventure in financial literacy and empowerment for your family. The journey towards financial wellness is ever-evolving, with new challenges and opportunities at every turn. While we've covered the critical aspects of understanding money, the roles within a family's financial ecosystem, and setting the stage for financial wellness, these are merely the first steps.

1. **For a Deeper Dive:** We've sprinkled various callouts and sidebars throughout this chapter, guiding you toward YourFamilyYourFinances.com. Here, you'll find abundant resources, further reading, and actionable advice to continue building upon the foundation we've started here.

2. **Bringing Concepts to Life:** Additionally, we've highlighted specific episodes of *Your Family Your Finances,* available at yfyf.YourHomeTV.com. These episodes are designed to complement the topics we've discussed, offering visual, relatable examples that bring financial concepts to life engagingly and understandably.

The Power of Family Engagement

Building a solid financial foundation is a journey best undertaken together as a family. The strategies and activities outlined in this chapter are merely starting points. Engaging as a family in regular discussions, collaborative decision-making, and shared learning experiences strengthens your financial foundation and reinforces the bonds that tie your family together.

Let curiosity and a shared desire for financial well-being drive your family's journey as you move forward. Encourage questions, celebrate achievements (no matter how small), and view setbacks as opportunities for growth and learning. The path to financial wellness is paved with knowledge, understanding, and action. Taking these first steps together lays the groundwork for a future where financial decisions are made confidently and collaboratively. Continue building on your knowledge, remain open to new ideas, and keep moving forward.

Here's to the beginning of a rewarding journey towards financial empowerment for your family. Let's make it a journey full of learning, growth, and shared success.

A financially healthy environment is like a garden; it needs care, nourishment, and regular attention to thrive.

Chapter 2

Budgeting Basics For The Family

"Budgeting is not just for people who don't have enough money. It is for everyone who wants to ensure that their money is enough for the life they want to live." - Unknown

Imagine setting sail on a vast ocean, navigating towards the island of your dreams. In this journey, budgeting is your compass, guiding you through the waves of financial uncertainty, toward your desired destination: financial well-being and freedom.

At its core, budgeting is about understanding and managing where your money comes from and where it's going. It's a proactive approach that empowers you and your family to make informed, conscious financial decisions. Think of it, not as a restriction, but as a tool for achieving your family's dreams: a comfortable home, quality education for your children, memorable vacations, or secure retirement.

Why Budget?

In a world brimming with financial obligations and temptations, a budget acts as a beacon, illuminating the path to financial stability and success. It enables you to:

- **Prioritize your spending:** Align your expenditures with your family's values and goals.

- **Avoid debt:** Live within your means and save for the future.

- **Feel in control:** Reduce financial stress by knowing exactly what's happening with your money.

Income Analysis: The Starting Point

The budgeting journey begins with a clear understanding of your family's income. It's not just about the regular paychecks, but also about every bit that adds to your financial pool: freelance work, side hustles, rental income, or any passive income streams.

Start by documenting every source of income, no matter how small. This comprehensive view is crucial for accurate budgeting. It will also serve as a guideline to determine ways to create additional income down the road. That will be the subject of a future book in this series around creating family income, but you need to know where you are starting from.

Note the regularity of each income source. Is it monthly, bi-weekly, or irregular? This understanding will help you plan your budget more effectively. As you budget in the future, try to keep your essential expenses paid for by regular sources of income instead of irregular. Use irregular income to pay for your discretionary expenses (i.e. "The Fun Stuff").

Expense Tracking: Navigating Your Expenditures

Equally important is tracking where your money goes each month. This involves distinguishing between fixed expenses (those that don't change much, like rent or mortgage) and **variable expenses** (those that can fluctuate, like groceries or entertainment).

- **Fixed Expenses:** These are your non-negotiables, the costs you must cover to maintain your family's lifestyle. Understanding these helps ensure you're always aware of the situation.

- **Variable Expenses:** These offer more flexibility but require mindfulness. By tracking these expenses, you can identify areas where adjustments can free up more money for savings or paying down debt.

The Power of Awareness

Awareness of spending patterns is the first step toward financial mastery. By knowing exactly where your money is going, you can make adjustments that align more closely with your family's financial goals and priorities. This awareness is empowering, turning seemingly small daily choices into significant milestones on your journey to financial wellness.

Creating a Family Budget

Creating a family budget is akin to drawing a map for a treasure hunt. It outlines the path to your financial goals, ensuring every dollar is directed with purpose. Here's how to start charting your course. Begin by identifying the categories that make up your family's budget. These categories should mirror your financial reality and aspirations, offering a clear view of where your money needs to go.

- **Essential Expenses:** These are your non-negotiables—housing, food, utilities, insurance, and education costs.

- **Savings Goals:** Prioritize categories for emergency funds, retirement savings, and other significant goals like college funds or home repairs.

- **Discretionary Spending:** This is for wants rather than needs—entertainment, dining out, and hobbies. While flexible, managing this category wisely is crucial to avoid overspending.

With your categories defined, the next step is allocating your income to cover each area. It's about finding a balance that supports your immediate needs and future dreams.

- **Fixed vs. Variable:** First, allocate funds to your fixed expenses, as these are typically consistent month-to-month. Then, allocate what remains to variable expenses and savings.

- **Percentage-Based Allocation:** Consider using percentage guidelines (e.g., the 50/30/20 rule: 50% on needs, 30% on wants, 20% on savings) as a starting point, adjusting as needed to fit your family's specific situation.

Adjusting for Seasonal Changes: Planning Ahead

A static budget is a common pitfall. Life changes, and so should your budget. Seasonal expenses can significantly impact your financial flow.

Building an effective budget considers predictable monthly expenses and those that occur only at certain times of the year. Identify upcoming seasonal expenses (holidays, back-to-school, vacations) and adjust your budget in advance. This might mean temporarily increasing the allocation to discretionary spending or savings in anticipation of these costs.

An extremely important part of any budget is ensuring you contribute to an Emergency Fund. Ensure that your budget includes building and maintaining an emergency fund to cover unexpected expenses without derailing your financial goals.

Activity: Crafting Your Family Budget Workshop

Gather the family for a budgeting workshop. You'll need a large sheet of paper or a digital spreadsheet, colored pens or markers, and a calculator.

1. **Draw Your Budget Pie Chart:** Draw a pie chart of your current budget using the categories you've defined. Allocate your income to each category based on your previous discussions and calculations.

2. **Discuss and Adjust:** As a family, discuss if the current allocations align with

your goals and values. Are there areas you can adjust to better meet your future aspirations?

3. **Plan for Seasonal Changes:** Mark the months with anticipated extra expenses on a calendar. Discuss how you can adjust your budget in these months to accommodate these costs without impacting your savings goals.

A family budget, created and agreed upon by all members, is a powerful tool for achieving financial wellness. It ensures that everyone is committed to the financial goals and understands their part in reaching them. Through regular reviews and adjustments, your family can confidently navigate the financial journey, prepared for both the expected and unexpected turns along the way.

Just as a ship requires the coordinated effort of its entire crew to navigate the seas successfully, a family needs the involvement of all its members to steer its financial journey toward prosperity. Here's how you can make budgeting a collaborative family endeavor.

Family Budget Meetings: A Cornerstone of Financial Unity

Regular family budget meetings are more than just discussions about numbers; they are a ritual that strengthens the fabric of family financial wellness. These meetings foster transparency, accountability, and collective problem-solving. They demystify financial processes for younger members and reinforce the family's financial goals and priorities.

Schedule monthly or quarterly meetings when everyone can be present without distractions. Create an agenda that includes reviewing the current budget, discussing upcoming expenses, and evaluating the progress toward savings goals.

Beyond keeping everyone on the same financial page, these meetings empower family members to voice their ideas and concerns, enhancing mutual respect and understanding.

Roles and Responsibilities: Everyone Plays a Part

Involving each family member in the budgeting process helps distribute the workload. It instills a sense of ownership and contribution towards the family's financial well-being.

- **For the Young Ones:** Assign simple, engaging tasks like tracking savings for a specific goal or choosing budget-friendly activities for family entertainment.

- **Teenagers:** Can take on more complex roles, such as managing a particular budget category (with guidance), or researching money-saving strategies for family expenses.

- **Adults:** Typically oversee the broader aspects of the budget, such as income management, bill payments, and savings allocations, but sharing these responsibilities can offer valuable learning opportunities for older children.

Family Budget Role-Play

Turn your next family budget meeting into a role-play session, where each member assumes a different financial role or responsibility than usual.

Write down various budgeting roles and tasks on slips of paper and have family members draw them randomly. If you do this each time you have a family budget meeting, that ensures that everyone has the opportunity to serve in different roles and will have the ability to learn.

This can either be adjusted for the young ones, or one of the adults or older children can help them. Allow each member to act out their assigned role, making decisions or suggestions based on their new perspective.

After the role-play, discuss what everyone learned from experiencing a different aspect of the family's finances. What insights did they gain? How might this affect your family's approach to budgeting?

By actively engaging in budgeting together, your family strengthens its financial foundation and builds a culture of open communication, mutual support, and shared responsibility. These meetings and activities are stepping stones toward a future where financial decisions are made collectively, with an understanding and respect for each person's perspective and contribution.

Engaging the family in budgeting isn't just about numbers; it's about nurturing a shared commitment to financial wellness and the dreams you're working together to achieve.

Through regular meetings and clear roles and responsibilities, every family member becomes a valued participant in the journey toward financial security and fulfillment.

Activity: Design Your Family Budget Night

Creating a family budget should feel like a smooth process. Transform your Family Budget Night into an engaging and memorable experience. Here's how to make it informative, interactive, and fun for everyone:

Step 1: Preparation Checklist

Before the big night, gather all the necessary tools and information to ensure a smooth and productive session:

- **Financial Statements:** Bank statements, pay stubs, bills, and any other documents that detail your income and expenses.

- **List of Expenses:** Write down or print out a list of your current monthly expenses, fixed (like rent or mortgage) and variable (like groceries or entertainment).

- **Budgeting Tools:** Whether you prefer digital apps, spreadsheets, or good old pen and paper, have your budgeting tools ready. Also, bring calculators for quick calculations.

- **Comfortable Setting:** Set a cozy space where everyone can sit together without distractions. Snacks and drinks can make the atmosphere more relaxed and welcoming.

Step 2: Discussion Prompts

Kick off your budget night with a round of open-ended questions to get everyone thinking and talking about finances. Here are a few prompts to start:

1. What are our family's financial goals for the next year? The next five years?

2. What expenses do we have coming up that we need to save for?

3. Are there areas where we can cut back our spending?

4. How can each of us contribute to our financial goals?

Step 3: Budgeting Game

Turn budget allocation into a game everyone can participate in and learn from. Here's a simple yet effective game to play:

- **The Allocation Game:** Create mock money using paper or monopoly money, representing your monthly income. Lay out jars or envelopes labeled with your budget categories (Housing, Food, Savings, Fun, etc.).

- **The Challenge:** Each family member takes turns allocating the mock money into the categories based on what they think is appropriate. After all the money is allocated, discuss where it went as a family and make adjustments as needed to ensure it aligns with your family's goals and needs.

- **Learning Outcome:** This game helps visualize how income is distributed across different expenses and savings, promoting discussions on prioritizing spending and the importance of saving.

Step 4: Wrap-Up - Reflect and Commit

End your budget night by reflecting on what was learned and committing to implementing the budget decided upon. Highlight the importance of teamwork and consistency in following the budget plan.

- **Next Steps:** Based on your discussion, assign tasks or follow-ups, such as researching cheaper service providers, setting up automatic savings transfers, or finding ways to increase income.

- **Schedule the Next Meeting:** Decide when to hold your next Family Budget Night to review your progress and make adjustments as necessary.

By turning budgeting into a collective and enjoyable activity, you teach valuable financial lessons and strengthen your family's teamwork and communication. Family Budget Night becomes an event that everyone can look forward to, where financial management becomes a shared journey toward achieving your family's dreams and goals.

Case Study: The Martinez Family's Budgeting Breakthrough

Meet the Martinez family: Laura and Miguel, with their two children, Sofia (15) and Luca (12). The Martinez family was doing okay financially, but they often stressed over unexpected expenses and struggled to save for vacations and college funds. They decided it was time for a change and committed to holding their first Family Budget Night.

Preparation and Approach

Laura and Miguel started by gathering all their financial statements and creating a list of their monthly expenses. They decided to use a simple spreadsheet for their budgeting tool, feeling it would be something both Sofia and Luca could easily understand and engage with.

For their budgeting game, they created paper money equal to their monthly income and labeled envelopes with their budget categories. They were ready to make budgeting a family affair.

Family Budget Night

The night began with Miguel asking, "What are some things we're saving for that really matter to us?" This question sparked a lively conversation, with Sofia expressing her dream of attending art school and Luca wanting to save for a new computer. They all agreed on setting aside money for a family vacation.

Each family member took turns placing paper money into the envelopes when playing the allocation game. Sofia was surprised to see how much went into necessities like rent and utilities. At the same time, Luca found it challenging to allocate enough to savings after covering all the expenses.

The game revealed that they spent a lot on dining out and barely used subscriptions. The family cut back on these areas to bolster their savings and vacation fund.

The Outcome

The Martinez family left their first budget night feeling more united and in control of their finances. They agreed to monthly check-ins, adjusting their budget as needed. Luca was responsible for tracking their dining expenses, and Sofia suggested creative ways to have fun without spending much.

This hands-on experience taught Sofia and Luca valuable lessons about budgeting and prioritizing. It showed them that financial wellness was a team effort that brought their family closer together and made their dreams seem more attainable.

Wrap-Up: Embracing Budgeting as a Continuous Journey

As we conclude our journey through the world of budgeting, it's essential to remember that this is not merely a chapter you read once and move on from. Budgeting is a living, breathing process that evolves alongside your family's needs, goals, and financial landscape. It's a compass that guides you through financial decisions, big and small, ensuring you're always heading toward your desired destination.

The path to mastering budgeting is one of continuous learning and engagement. As your family grows and changes, so will your budgeting strategies and priorities. This journey is best navigated with an open mind and a willingness to adapt.

- **A Wealth of Resources:** www.YourFamilyYourFinances.com/playbook-resources stands ready to support you on this journey, offering an ever-growing repository of budgeting resources. From downloadable templates and interactive tools, to in-depth articles and personal stories, there's something for everyone looking to deepen their budgeting knowledge and skills.

- **Bringing Budgeting to Life:** For those who prefer visual and practical examples, yfyf.YourHomeTV.com features relevant episodes of *Your Family Your Finances* that delve into budgeting topics. These episodes complement the guidance provided in this playbook, offering real-life insight and strategies to enhance your budgeting practice.

Celebrating Every Step

Much like any aspect of personal finance, budgeting is a journey marked by successes and learning opportunities. Celebrate your victories, no matter how small they may seem. Successfully sticking to your grocery budget, finding creative ways to save on utilities, or simply having a productive family budget meeting are all milestones worth acknowledging.

At the same time, setbacks should be viewed, not as failures, but as valuable lessons and opportunities for growth. Each challenge encountered is a chance to refine your approach, learn more about your financial habits, and strengthen your resolve to achieve your family's financial goals.

Looking Ahead

As you move forward, keep the dialogue around budgeting open and active within your family. Regularly review and adjust your budget, involve family members in financial decisions, and never shy away from exploring new strategies or tools that could enhance your financial wellness.

Budgeting is more than numbers on a spreadsheet; it's a shared commitment to a future of financial stability and fulfillment. By embracing budgeting as an ongoing process and engaging with the resources available, your family can build a solid financial foundation to support your dreams and aspirations for years to come.

Remember, the budgeting journey is one best traveled together, with each step bringing you closer to realizing the financial wellness and freedom your family deserves.

At its core, budgeting is about understanding and managing where your money comes from and where it's going

Chapter 3

Smart Spending Habits

"Too many people spend money they haven't earned to buy things they don't want, to impress people they don't like." - Will Rogers

Welcome to a chapter that could change how you view every dollar that flows through your family's hands. Smart spending isn't just about tightening belts and cutting corners; it's about making every cent work for you, bringing you closer to your financial dreams while allowing for joy and satisfaction in the present.

The Art of Smart Spending

At its heart, smart spending is about informed choices. It's recognizing that money is a limited resource and using it in ways that align with your family's values, needs, and long-term goals. This approach strikes a healthy balance between frugality and deprivation, ensuring that while you're cautious about your expenditures, you're not stripping your life of happiness and contentment.

Visibility is Key: Tracking and Categorizing

The journey to smart spending begins with visibility. You can't manage what you don't measure. Here's how to start.

Dedicate monthly time to tracking where your money goes. Use apps, spreadsheets, or pen and paper—whatever works best for your family. Everyone in the family should participate in this process. Being open about where money is being spent helps everyone understand and eliminates some of the "I want" discussions.

Divide your expenses into categories (e.g., housing, food, entertainment). This step is crucial for identifying areas where adjustments can be made for smarter spending. It is also helpful for gaining a better perspective on your spending habits. Are you spending more on entertainment than you usually do? Have you had major expenses that you did not anticipate? It is not always about cutting expenses but learning how your cash flow works so that you can anticipate expenses.

Needs vs. Wants: The Cornerstone of Financial Decision-Making

One of the most transformative skills you can develop is differentiating between needs and wants:

- **Needs:** These are essentials, things you can't (or shouldn't) live without—food, shelter, healthcare, and education.

- **Wants:** These are nice to have but not essential. Wants include dining out, the latest gadgets, and luxury items.

You will want to ask, "Is this purchase essential for our well-being or happiness? Can we achieve our goal without it?" This process helps align spending with your family's true priorities. E-commerce has made our lives easier, but this is not always good. Easy means that it is very **easy** to overspend. One of the techniques I use now with my Amazon account is to put things that are not immediate essentials, I put them in my cart and leave them there for a few days before I complete the transaction. It is amazing how often I go back in and forget to put it in there.

By embracing smart spending habits, you're safeguarding your finances and teaching your family the value of money and the importance of making thoughtful decisions. This chapter will guide you through understanding your spending patterns, making those crucial distinctions between needs and wants, and ultimately spending smarter—not harder.

Creating a Conscious Spending Plan

Crafting a conscious spending plan is akin to charting a course through the financial seas, ensuring your family's ship stays afloat and sails smoothly toward your goals. This section explores strategies for allocating your financial resources wisely and adopting a flexible approach to budgeting. The essence of a conscious spending plan lies in its ability to prioritize how financial resources are distributed, ensuring that every dollar spent or saved serves a purpose.

The first step in the process is to prioritize the essentials. Begin with the non-negotiables: housing, utilities, food, and healthcare. These essentials form the foundation of your budget and ensure your family's basic needs are met. That does not mean you can't look for ways to reduce some of these costs. Look at areas like insurance, trips to the grocery store, and setting back the thermostats when no one is home as ways to reduce the costs of some of these essentials.

Once essentials are covered, the next slice of your financial pie should go towards savings. This includes your emergency fund, retirement savings, and specific goals like education or vacation savings. Instilling a "save first" mentality is crucial for long-term financial health.

What remains can be allocated to wants and discretionary spending. However, even this spending should be done with intention, focusing on activities and purchases that bring genuine joy and value to your family.

Embracing Flexible Budgeting

Life is anything but static, and your budget should reflect that. Flexible budgeting allows you to adjust spending categories as needed, responding to life's inevitable changes and opportunities.

Setting some money aside for the unexpected should be a priority. Allocate a portion of your budget each month for unforeseen expenses. If unused, it can roll over into savings or future discretionary spending.

That said, you also need to be able to adapt to what life throws at you. Whether it's an unexpected car repair, a sudden job loss, or a happy occasion like a family celebration, having a flexible budget means you can adjust without derailing your financial goals.

Make it a habit to review your budget monthly. This regular check-in is the perfect time to adjust allocations based on past spending and anticipated changes, ensuring your budget reflects your family's needs and priorities.

A conscious spending plan, underpinned by wise allocation and flexibility, is more than just a budget—it's a declaration of your family's financial values and a roadmap to achieving your dreams. Regularly revisiting and adjusting this plan ensures that your family's financial journey is intentional and adaptable, ready to confidently meet whatever the future holds.

Teaching Children About Spending

Teaching children about spending is an investment in their future financial well-being. By integrating lessons on money management into their daily lives, you're not just talking about numbers, you're instilling values and skills that will serve them for life.

Allowances and Spending Decisions

Allowances can be a powerful tool in teaching children about spending, saving, and understanding the value of money. Here's how to make the most of this educational opportunity:

- **Consistent Allowance Schedule:** Whether weekly or monthly, a consistent allowance gives children a sense of predictability and responsibility. It's their money to manage within the guidelines you set together.

- **Spend, Save, Give:** Encourage dividing the allowance into three parts: spending on immediate wants, saving for larger goals, and giving to charity or saving for a family project. This teaches budgeting, patience, and generosity.

- **Real-Life Decisions:** Use allowance as a basis for real-life spending decisions. If your child wants a new toy or game, discuss the cost and how they can save their allowance to purchase it. This emphasizes the value of money and the satisfaction of earning and saving for what they want.

Engaging Activities: Learning Through Doing

Involving children in family financial decisions and activities educates them about spending and makes the learning process fun and memorable.

- **Budget-Friendly Family Outing:** Plan a family outing with a set budget. Involve the children in researching and choosing activities that fit within the budget and discussing costs and value. It's a practical way to teach them to make spending decisions considering enjoyment and financial constraints.

- **Price Comparison Game:** Turn grocery shopping into a learning experience by making a game out of finding the best deals. Challenge your children to compare prices and determine which options offer the best value for money. This teaches them about smart shopping practices and the impact of spending decisions on a budget.

- **DIY Project Fund:** Start a small fund for a DIY home project, like redecorating a room or building a backyard garden. Involve the children in budgeting for materials and making spending decisions. This activity teaches them about managing money for larger projects and the rewards of hard work and planning.

Teaching children about spending through allowances and engaging in activities is more than just financial education; it gives them the tools to navigate the world confidently and fully. These lessons in money management, when started early and reinforced through practical experiences, lay the foundation for a lifetime of smart spending habits and financial literacy.

Family Activity: Family Spending Diary Review

A spending diary review can be an enlightening activity for fostering financial awareness and smart spending habits within your family. This project encourages each family member to track their spending over a set period, leading to a shared discussion about financial habits and how they align with your family's values and goals.

Setup: Tracking Your Spending

1. **Choose Your Tool:** Decide as a family whether you'll use digital apps, a simple notebook, or a spreadsheet for tracking spending. Each member should use the same method for consistency in the review process.

2. **Define the Period:** A month is ideal for tracking spending, providing a comprehensive view of where money goes in a typical cycle of bills and activities.

3. **Categories:** Set up categories that reflect your family's typical expenses. These might include food, entertainment, personal items, savings, etc. Encourage everyone to record even small purchases.

Conducting a Reflection Session

After the tracking period, schedule a family meeting to discuss your findings. This reflection session is not about judgment but understanding and improving.

1. **Share Findings:** Each family member presents their spending diary, highlighting their observations. Focus on emerging patterns, such as unexpected expenses, frequent small purchases, or areas where savings could be achieved.

2. **Discuss Insights:** Discuss what these spending habits reveal about your priorities and whether they align with your family's financial goals. This is an excellent opportunity to reinforce the concept of needs vs. wants.

3. **Identify Changes:** Decide on one or two specific changes each person can make to improve their spending habits. This could be as simple as making coffee at home instead of buying it, or setting a weekly limit for personal spending.

Implementing Changes

1. **Action Plan:** Create a simple action plan for the changes agreed upon. Assign accountability partners within the family to help keep each other on track.

2. **Follow-Up:** Schedule a follow-up meeting, perhaps a month later, to review the impact of these changes. Have spending habits improved? Are there new insights or adjustments to be made?

The Family Spending Diary Review is more than just an exercise in tracking expenses; it's a powerful tool for building financial literacy and fostering open communication about money within your family. By reflecting on spending habits together, you can make collective strides towards smarter spending that supports your family's broader financial goals and dreams. This activity not only reveals each member's spending habits but also encourages a collaborative approach to financial planning and problem-solving, reinforcing the idea that managing finances is a shared responsibility and journey.

Case Study: The Thompson Family's Spending Diary Journey

Meet the Thompsons: Mia, Leo, and their two children, Sarah (13) and Ethan (10). Like many families, they occasionally needed clarification about where their money was going each month. Despite having a budget, they often encountered surprises that threw their plans off course. They decided to undertake a family project: keeping a spending diary for one month to gain insights into their spending habits.

The Setup

The Thompsons agreed to track every penny spent for an entire month. They chose a simple spreadsheet for Leo and Mia. At the same time, Sarah and Ethan received notebooks, turning the task into a fun project. They categorized expenses into necessities, education, entertainment, and savings, ensuring a comprehensive view of their financial flow.

Tracking in Action

Each family member enthusiastically took to the task. Ethan, initially reluctant, found joy in jotting down his small purchases, realizing how often he asked for money for snacks after school. Sarah discovered she was spending more than she thought on app purchases. Mia and Leo noticed patterns in their grocery shopping and dining out expenses that they hadn't fully acknowledged.

The Reflection Session

After a month, the Thompsons gathered around the living room with their spending diaries and spreadsheets. They discussed their findings openly, focusing not on blame but on understanding and improving. They discovered that dining out was a significant expense, motivated more by convenience than enjoyment. They also saw opportunities to plan grocery shopping better to avoid last-minute, expensive trips.

Insights and Changes

The family decided on two major changes:

- **Dining In:** They agreed to limit dining out to once a week, planning it as a family event to make it more memorable. Mia and Sarah volunteered to find new recipes at home, making cooking a family activity.

- **Smart Grocery Shopping:** Leo and Ethan created a weekly meal plan to streamline grocery shopping, aiming to reduce waste and impulse buys.

The Outcome

The Thompsons met again a month after implementing these changes to review their progress. They were pleasantly surprised by the savings from dining in and more efficient grocery shopping. The children felt proud of their contributions, and the family enjoyed their time cooking and eating together more than they expected.

This exercise helped the Thompsons improve their spending habits and brought them closer as a family. They learned the value of tracking expenses and making conscious decisions about their spending. The spending diary project became a valuable life lesson for Sarah and Ethan, showing them the importance of mindfulness in financial matters.

The Thompson family's journey with a spending diary illuminates the power of tracking expenses and reflecting on spending habits as a family. It's a testament to how a simple activity can lead to significant insights and positive changes, reinforcing the value of smart spending habits in achieving financial goals and fostering family unity.

Wrap-Up: The Path to Smart Spending

As we close this chapter, it's crucial to remember that the journey towards smart spending is ongoing and ever-evolving. The steps you've taken and the lessons you've learned are merely the beginning of a broader adventure in financial stewardship for your family.

As we transition into the next chapter, we will apply the skills we developed through smart spending habits to your family savings strategy. This will be a tool that once mastered will begin to create wealth for your family going forward.

Chapter 4

Mastering The Art Of Saving

"A penny saved is a penny earned." - Benjamin Franklin

Imagine standing at the edge of a serene lake, pebbles in hand. With each pebble tossed into the water, ripples expand outward, reaching further than the point of impact. In the realm of personal finance, saving is akin to those pebbles, a seemingly small act that sets forth waves of security, opportunity, and growth that touch all corners of your family's future.

The Transformative Power of Saving

Saving, at its essence, is the act of setting aside money today for future use. It's a cornerstone habit that not only shores financial stability but also opens doors to dreams and aspirations once deemed out of reach. Whether buying a home, funding an education, or planning a dream vacation, saving transforms these dreams from mere wisps of imagination into tangible realities.

Unlike investing, which entails putting your money to work in hopes of generating a return, saving is about preservation and accumulation. It's the bedrock upon which the edifice of financial wellness is built, providing a buffer against life's uncertainties and a launchpad for future ventures.

Why Save?

In a world where immediate gratification is often a click away, the discipline of saving might seem out of step with the times. Yet, the benefits of this foundational financial habit are both immediate and far-reaching:

- **Security:** An emergency fund, one of the primary goals of saving, offers a financial safety net that can help your family weather unexpected storms without derailing your long-term financial plans.

- **Freedom:** Savings allow you to make choices that align with your family's values and goals without the constraints imposed by financial pressures.

- **Peace of Mind:** Knowing you have a financial cushion can reduce stress and anxiety, contributing to overall well-being and happiness.

- **Empowerment:** Regular saving practices empower your family to take control of your financial destiny, setting the stage for more complex financial strategies, including investing.

Laying the Foundation

As we delve deeper into the art of saving, we'll explore strategies for building and maintaining your savings, setting achievable goals, and making saving a family affair. Through this journey, you'll discover that saving is not just about stashing money away; it's about creating a future rich in possibilities and free from financial constraints. Embrace saving as a transformative power in your family's life. Let it be the steady hand that guides your financial decisions, the foundation upon which you build your dreams, and the legacy you pass on to your children. Welcome to the art of saving—a journey of security, opportunity, and growth.

At the heart of saving lies a fundamental psychological challenge: the battle between immediate gratification and long-term well-being. Understanding the difference between needs and wants is crucial in this area. Needs are essentials, the non-negotiables for survival, and basic comfort. At the same time, wants are the extras, the nice-to-haves that make life enjoyable, but are not essential for our day-to-day existence.

The concept of delayed gratification plays a pivotal role in saving. It's the ability to resist the temptation of an immediate reward in preference for a later, often greater, reward.

Saving for a future goal usually means forgoing smaller, immediate pleasures in favor of larger, long-term aspirations.

It is important to develop the skill of differentiating your needs from wants. This differentiation is not just about making financial decisions; it's about self-awareness and control. It requires asking yourself whether a purchase is essential for your well-being or if it's a desire that can be postponed or even discarded, allowing you to deploy that money to savings instead.

Cultivating a Saving Mindset

Developing a mindset that prioritizes saving is akin to training for a marathon. It requires preparation, discipline, and a clear vision of the finish line. Visualizing your financial goals can be a powerful motivator. Picture what achieving these goals looks and feels like. Whether you want to own a home, ensure a comfortable retirement, or provide for your children's education, keeping these images at the forefront can help reinforce your saving habits.

Once you have visualized your financial goals, it is time to write them down. Goals should be specific, measurable, achievable, relevant, and time-bound (SMART). Instead of a vague goal like "save more money," aim for something concrete: "save $5000 for an emergency fund by the end of the year." This specificity makes the goal more tangible and motivating.

Recognize and celebrate milestones along the way. Saving is a journey, and acknowledging progress, no matter how small, can boost motivation and encourage us to keep going. This is a way to keep savings a fun process instead of something that feels negative.

Overcoming Psychological Barriers

Saving isn't just a financial activity; it's a mental one. The journey to a robust saving habit can be fraught with psychological barriers, including the fear of missing out (FOMO), societal pressures to spend, and the challenge of breaking established spending habits. Remind yourself of your long-term goals and their reasons. Social media and peer pressure can amplify the desire for immediate gratification, but staying focused on your personal financial journey is key.

View saving, not as a sacrifice, but as a positive step towards financial freedom and achieving your dreams. Changing your narrative around saving can transform it from a chore to a rewarding part of your life. Understanding the psychological underpinnings of saving and cultivating a mindset that embraces delayed gratification, differentiates between needs and wants, and sets clear, motivating goals that are essential to mastering the art of saving. Families can build a solid foundation for financial stability, and realize their dreams by navigating these mental landscapes with intention and purpose.

Saving Strategies for Families

In the journey of saving, consistency is key. Automating your savings is one of the most effective ways to ensure your family stays on track. Setting up automatic transfers to your savings account removes the mental load and the temptation to spend what you've intended to save. It's like putting your savings on autopilot. In today's high-tech world, banks, savings and loans, and even direct deposit from your paycheck make it extremely easy to establish and manage automated savings.

Most banks offer the option to set up automatic transfers from your checking account to your savings account. Decide on an amount that fits your budget, and schedule it right after your payday, ensuring savings are your highest priority.

Choosing the Right Savings Account: Maximizing Growth

Not all savings accounts are created equal, especially regarding interest rates. A high-interest savings account can significantly enhance your family's savings growth over time. Look for accounts offering competitive interest rates. Even a slight difference can add up to a considerable amount over the years. Shop for these types of accounts by comparing savings rates on sites like NerdWallet (www.nerdwallet.com) or Bankrate.com (www.bankrate.com).

Due to lower overhead costs, online banks often offer higher interest rates than traditional brick-and-mortar banks. Don't overlook these options when searching for the best place to grow your savings. All of these types of banks will offer the ability to deposit checks through a phone app. They will also offer the ability to link to your checking account via the Automated Clearing House (ACH) so that you can easily and affordably move money between banks.

Building an Emergency Fund: Your Financial Safety Net

An emergency fund is essential for any family's financial stability. It's your buffer against the unexpected, ensuring you're prepared for life's inevitable surprises.

Setting a modest goal for your emergency fund—$1,000 is a good starting point. This can cover minor emergencies and help you avoid debt. Later in the book, we will discuss strategies for determining a proper emergency fund.

Once you've reached your initial goal, aim to develop an emergency fund to cover 3-6 months' worth of living expenses. This will provide a more substantial safety net for job loss or significant medical costs.

Your emergency fund should be easily accessible but not too easy to dip into for non-emergencies. Consider a high-yield savings account that offers liquidity and growth. It should be accessible but not too easy so you don't raid it for non-emergencies.

In figure 4.1 below, we illustrated the difference between a 2% and a 5% savings rate over time. At the time this book was written, it was not unusual to find this difference in interest rates from local banks and online high-yield savings. Take a look at the difference in total savings over time with just a 3% difference.

Figure 4.1

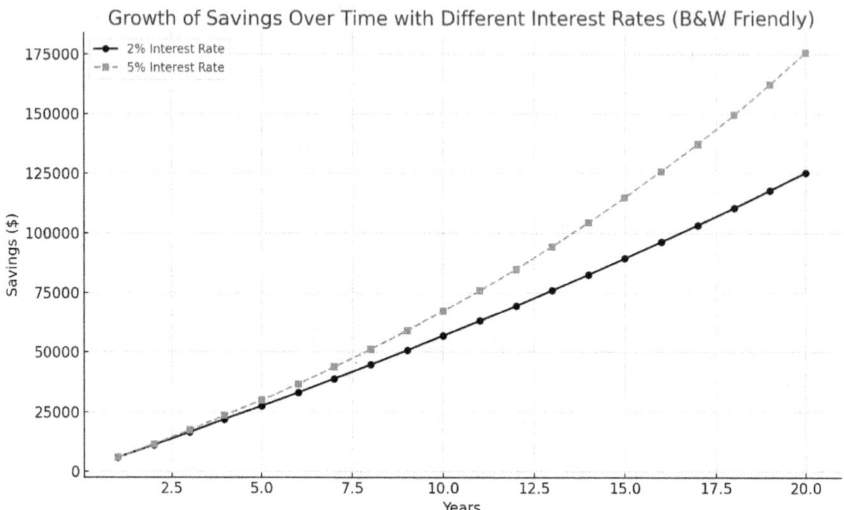

Figure 4.1: The chart illustrates savings growth over time, comparing the impact of two interest rates: 2% and 5%. The initial savings amount to $1000, with an annual deposit of $5000 over 20 years.

However, it is not just the interest rate that will dramatically affect our savings over time. Consistency is also important. Is it better to contribute the same amount of money per month or to put in what you can afford each month? Let's take a look.

Figure 4.2

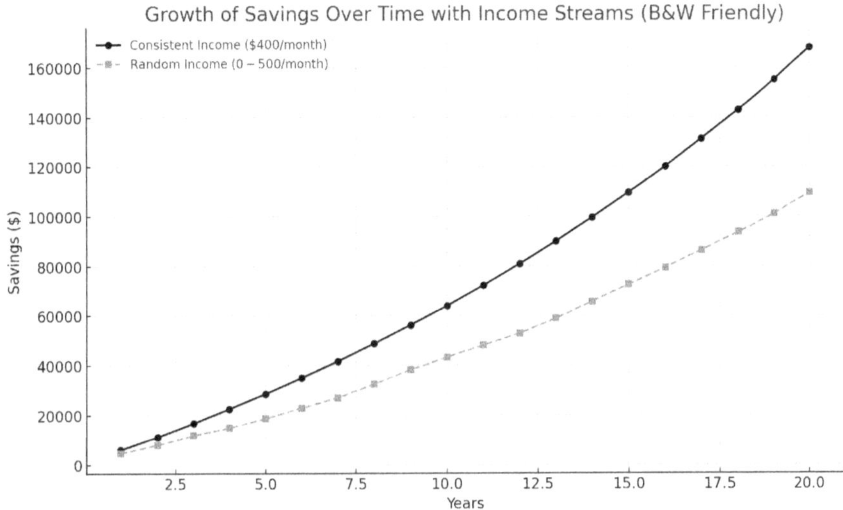

Figure 4.2: The chart illustrates the growth of savings over time, at 5%, with two different savings streams. The first savings strategy is a consistent monthly deposit of $400 per month for 20 years. The second deposit strategy is based on a random series of monthly deposits from $0 to $500 per month over 20 years. The initial savings amount is $1000.

As you can see in figure 4.2, a strategy of consistent deposits over time tends to give you better results. As you build your savings strategy, you certainly want to be aware of the rate of interest that you are earning. Still, even more importantly, you want to be consistent with that strategy. This is an excellent case for using an automated savings strategy.

Adopting these saving strategies can transform your family's financial future. Automating savings ensures consistent growth, choosing high-interest accounts maximizes your money's potential, and building an emergency fund secures your financial well-being against unforeseen challenges.

Together, these practices lay a solid foundation for achieving your family's dreams and aspirations, proving that saving is not just about setting money aside—it's about creating a brighter future.

Involving the Whole Family in Saving

Saving becomes more meaningful and effective when it's a collective family effort. Setting both collective and individual saving goals helps achieve financial milestones and strengthens family bonds through shared aspirations.

Start with a family meeting to discuss and decide on a big saving goal. Whether saving for a family vacation, a new car, or a renovation project, having a common objective unites the family with a shared purpose. Consider everyone's input to ensure the goal reflects the whole family's desires and priorities.

Encourage each family member to set personal saving goals too. For children, this could be saving for a new toy, book, or a special outing. This teaches them the value of money and the satisfaction of reaching a goal through persistence and saving.

Journeying Together: Tracking Progress

Monitoring your saving progress is crucial to staying motivated and on track. Here are some family-friendly methods to keep everyone engaged and excited about the saving journey:

- **Visual Charts:** Create a large chart or board that tracks progress toward your family's saving goals. Place it where everyone can see it daily. Use stickers, markers, or other creative ways to update and celebrate progress.

- **Saving Apps:** Many apps are designed to help track savings goals. Choose one, allowing multiple users so each family member can update their progress. This can also be a fun way for kids to engage with their personal saving goals digitally.

- **Regular Family Meetings:** Schedule monthly savings check-ins, during which the family can review progress together, discuss any challenges, and celebrate milestones. These meetings reinforce commitment to the goals and allow for adjustments as needed.

Saving Goal Poster Creation

Gather your family for a creative session to make a Saving Goal Poster. You'll need poster paper, markers, stickers, and any other craft supplies that you like.

- **Outline Your Goals:** Start by writing your collective and individual saving goals on the poster. Then, let everyone decorate a section of the poster related to their personal goals.

- **Progress Markers:** Create a way to mark progress visually on the poster. This could be a thermometer drawing for each goal you color in as you save more or a path leading to a goal where you move a marker forward with each saving milestone.

- **Place of Pride:** Hang the poster in a common area, which will serve as a daily reminder of your family's saving goals and progress.

Involving the whole family in setting and achieving savings goals transforms saving from a solitary task into a shared journey. It's about more than just reaching financial targets; it's about teaching valuable life lessons, fostering a sense of accomplishment, and creating lasting memories together. As you track your progress and celebrate each milestone, you'll find that the act of saving itself becomes a rewarding part of your family's story.

Family Activity: Family saving challenge

The Family Saving Challenge transforms saving from a mundane task into an exciting family adventure. This engaging activity promotes saving and teaches valuable lessons about teamwork, goal-setting, and the joy of achieving financial milestones together.

1. **Set a Collective Short-term Goal:** As a family, choose a savings goal that can be achieved relatively quickly—think a month or two. This could be saving for a family game night, a new board game everyone can enjoy, or a special family outing.

2. **Determine the Saving Amount:** Based on your budget, decide how much money your family needs to save to reach the goal. Make sure it's realistic and achievable within the set timeframe.

3. **Create a Challenge Tracker:** Visualize your progress by creating a tracker. This could be a chart on a poster, a jar where you add a physical token for each dollar saved, or a digital tracker if your family prefers tech solutions.

Assigning Roles and Tasks

Tailor roles and tasks to each family member's age, interests, and abilities to ensure everyone can actively participate and contribute:

- **Young Children:** Task them to find coins around the house or save a portion of their allowance.

- **Teenagers:** Can take on more substantial roles, like researching and suggesting ways the family can cut back on expenses or take on additional chores for extra allowance to contribute to the savings goal.

- **Adults:** Lead by example by identifying larger cost-saving opportunities or additional income sources. Also, manage the overall tracking and encouragement of the family's progress.

Rewards: Celebrating Together

Choosing meaningful, non-monetary rewards for reaching your saving goal reinforces the value of teamwork and the satisfaction of achieving financial milestones:

- **A Special Family Experience:** Whether it's a movie night at home with homemade popcorn and a favorite film, a camping trip in the backyard, or a DIY spa day, select a reward that brings joy and togetherness to your family.

- **A Certificate of Achievement:** Create personalized certificates for each family member, acknowledging their contribution to the saving challenge. This celebrates the achievement and is a tangible reminder of their hard work and dedication.

- **An Extra Vote:** For the next family decision-making event (like choosing the next movie to watch or the destination for your next outing), give each family member an extra vote or say in the decision as a reward for their efforts in the saving challenge.

The Family Saving Challenge is more than just a way to save money; it's an opportunity to come together as a family, work towards a common goal, and enjoy the fruits of your collective effort. By participating in this challenge, each family member learns the importance of saving, the value of teamwork, and the joy of achieving goals together. These lessons and shared experiences ultimately contribute to a strong, financially savvy family foundation.

Case Study: The Patel Family's Saving Challenge

Meet the Patel family: Priya and Amit, with their two children, Arjun (12) and Siya (8). The Patels were a typical family, trying to balance the day-to-day expenses while dreaming of bigger things like a summer vacation and enhancing their home entertainment system. They realized they needed to get serious about saving to achieve their dreams. Inspired by the idea of making saving a family affair, they decided to embark on a Family Saving Challenge.

Setting the Stage

The Patels convened a family meeting to discuss their saving goals. After some discussion, they agreed their short-term goal was to fund a new home entertainment system, which would allow for memorable family movie nights and gaming sessions. They calculated they needed to save $500 over the next three months.

Roles and Tasks

- **Priya** researched and compared prices for the entertainment system, ensuring they got the best deal once they reached their goal.

- **Amit**, an amateur chef, prepared more meals at home, reducing the family's dining out expenses.

- **Arjun** committed to washing the family car at home instead of going to the car wash, saving additional money towards the goal.

- **Siya** made greeting cards for upcoming family birthdays instead of buying them.

Tracking Progress

The Patels created a colorful chart to track their savings. They placed it on the refrigerator, where everyone could see and update it. They added to the chart each week, visibly marking their progress toward the $500 goal.

Rewards and Results

The family agreed that once they reached their goal, the first movie night with the new entertainment system would be a "Siya and Arjun Picks Night," with the kids choosing the movies and games for the evening. After three months of diligent saving and teamwork, the Patels reached their goal. Purchasing the entertainment system became a significant family milestone, celebrated with a fun-filled movie and gaming night. The challenge taught them valuable lessons about saving, teamwork, and the joy of achieving goals together.

Reflecting on the Journey

The Saving Challenge brought the Patel family closer and transformed their approach to finances. Arjun and Siya learned firsthand the value of money and the satisfaction of contributing to a family goal. Priya and Amit saw a marked improvement in their financial habits, realizing that saving for something specific made the process more tangible and rewarding.

The success of their first challenge inspired the Patels to continue setting family saving goals. They now looked forward to their monthly family finance meetings, where they could plan their next adventures, financial goals, or family outings.

The Patel family's journey underscores the transformative power of collaborative saving. By turning financial goals into a family project, the Patels achieved their objectives. They instilled in each family member the principles of saving, cooperation, and the joy of shared success.

Wrap-Up: The Empowerment of Saving

As we close this chapter on mastering the art of saving, let's reflect on the transformative journey we've embarked upon. Saving is more than accumulating money; it's about empowering your family to reach its dreams, withstand life's surprises, and build a foundation for future aspirations.

This journey of saving is both an individual and a collective family endeavor, weaving together the threads of discipline, teamwork, and achievement into the fabric of your family's life.

In the next chapter, we will help you and your family learn to set goals. You will see how that skill intertwines with every part of your financial and personal life.

Chapter 5

Setting and Achieving Financial Goals

"Setting goals is the first step in turning the invisible into the visible. But it's achieving those goals that transform the possible into the reality of our financial future." - Tony Robbins.

Embarking on a journey without a destination can be an adventure, but when it comes to your family's financial journey, having a clear roadmap is essential. This roadmap comprises financial goals, the beacons that guide your path through life's financial landscape. Setting these goals is the first step toward achieving financial security and realizing your family's dreams.

The Significance of Financial Goals

Financial goals are the foundation for your family's financial plans. They are not just about numbers or milestones but are deeply intertwined with your family's aspirations, dreams, and quality of life. Whether it's buying a home, saving for your children's education, planning for retirement, or simply taking a dream vacation, each goal reflects your family's values, priorities, and stages in life.

The beauty of financial goals lies in their diversity. They vary widely among families and even within a family over time. Here's a glimpse into how these goals can evolve:

- **Short-Term Goals:** These are the stepping stones and goals you aim to achieve within a year or two. Consider saving for a family vacation, building an emergency fund, or paying off a small debt. Short-term goals often boost confidence, providing tangible proof of your financial progress.

- **Medium-Term Goals:** Spanning a horizon of two to five years, medium-term goals bridge the gap between immediate satisfaction and long-term aspirations. Saving for a down payment on a home or funding a significant home improvement project might fall into this category.

- **Long-Term Goals:** These are the pillars of your family's financial plan, often extending five years or more into the future. Long-term goals include saving for retirement, your children's college education, or financial independence.

Reflecting Life Stages, Values, and Priorities

What sets your family's financial goals apart is how they reflect your unique life stages, values, and priorities. A young family might prioritize saving for a home or children's education. At the same time, those closer to retirement may focus on securing a comfortable future. Regardless of the stage, each goal is a step toward fulfilling your family's dreams and aspirations.

Setting financial goals is more than a financial exercise; it's a declaration of your family's hopes and dreams. As we delve deeper into this chapter, remember that these goals are your family's roadmap to financial security and the life you dream of. With careful planning, dedication, and the right strategies, these goals are not just possible—they're within reach.

Types of Financial Goals

Understanding the spectrum of financial goals is crucial in charting a course toward financial security and realizing your family's dreams. These goals can be considered stepping stones or milestones along your family's financial journey, varying in scope and timeline. Let's break down these goals into three primary categories: short-term, medium-term, and long-term.

Short-term Goals: Immediate Horizons

You aim to achieve short-term financial goals within a year or less. These are often the goals that cater to immediate needs or wants, serving as the building blocks for more extensive financial planning. Examples include:

- **Saving for a Vacation:** Allocating monthly funds to afford a family holiday without dipping into savings or accruing debt.

- **Building an Emergency Fund:** Starting with a modest aim of $1,000 to cover unexpected expenses, such as car repairs or medical bills.

- **Major Purchases:** Setting aside money for significant but necessary purchases, like a new appliance or computer.

Medium-term Goals: Planning Ahead

You plan to achieve medium-term financial goals within one to five years. They often involve more substantial financial commitments and require disciplined saving and planning. Examples include:

- **Down Payment for a Home:** Saving for a 20% down payment on a house is a goal that demands strategic savings and budget adjustments.

- **Renovation Projects:** Accumulating funds for significant home improvements or renovations that can enhance your living space and increase your home's value.

Long-term Goals: The Bigger Picture

Long-term financial goals span over five years and usually align with your family's most significant life aspirations. Achieving these goals requires patience, perseverance, and often investing. Examples include:

- **Retirement Savings:** Contributing to retirement accounts to ensure financial security in later years, recognizing the power of compound interest over time.

- **Children's Education Funds:** Saving for your children's college education is a goal that often involves exploring various savings and investment options, like

529 plans.

- **Financial Independence:** Many people's ultimate goal is financial independence, which means having enough savings, investments, and passive income to afford their desired lifestyle without needing to work full-time.

Differentiating between short-term, medium-term, and long-term financial goals helps families organize their financial planning efforts. This ensures a balanced approach that caters to immediate needs while paving the way for future aspirations. By recognizing and planning for these various goals, families can create a comprehensive financial roadmap that aligns with their life stages, values, and priorities, setting the stage for a secure and fulfilling future.

Strategies for Setting Goals

To transform financial dreams into achievable realities, families need a roadmap—a clear, structured approach to setting and pursuing financial goals. This section delves into practical strategies that clarify these goals and enhance their attainability.

Crafting SMART Financial Goals

The SMART framework provides a proven goal-setting structure that amplifies focus, clarity, and success. Here's how to apply it to your family's financial goals:

- **Specific:** Clearly define what you want to achieve. Instead of "save money," aim to "save $3,000 for an emergency fund."

- **Measurable:** Include precise amounts and dates to track progress. "Save $250 monthly towards the emergency fund" is measurable and provides clear checkpoints.

- **Achievable:** Ensure the goal is realistic, given your family's resources and commitments. Overambitious goals can lead to frustration and demotivation.

- **Relevant:** The goal should align with your family's broader financial plans and values. Saving for a home renovation should enhance your living situation or increase your home's value.

- **Time-bound:** Set a deadline. "Save $3,000 for an emergency fund within 12 months" gives a clear timeline that motivates action.

Visualizing Success: Keeping Goals in Focus

Visual tools like vision boards can be powerful motivators for keeping financial goals at the forefront of one's mind. By representing your goals visually, you can maintain your motivation and create an emotional connection to the goals.

A vision board displayed in a common area reminds everyone of the shared objectives, keeping the momentum alive. Take the opportunity throughout the weeks and months to reflect on where you are toward those goals on the vision board to keep the motivation to succeed. Visual depictions of goals (such as a photograph of a potential vacation destination) can strengthen emotional commitment to the saving process. The more real you can make it, the more the emotional connection to the goal. **Everyone** in the family should participate, not just the parents or the children.

Prioritizing Goals: Making Strategic Choices

When resources are limited, not all goals can simultaneously be pursued with equal vigor. Prioritizing becomes essential. As a result you will sometimes need to ask which goals will have the most significant positive impact on your family's life? These should generally take precedence. You will get to the other goals later.

It is also important to balance the short—and long-term goals, much like you are doing with the positive impact goals above. You will need to prioritize the time horizon. While long-term goals like retirement savings are critical, don't overlook short-term objectives that can improve your current quality of life or prevent financial stress.

As we discussed in the budgeting and spending chapters, you must be flexible about your goals. Be prepared to reassess and adjust priorities as your family's circumstances and goals evolve.

Activity: Family Goals Workshop

Conduct a family workshop to apply these strategies. Gather supplies for a vision board, list your financial goals, and categorize them using the SMART criteria. Discuss and decide which goals are most important, then create a visual representation to keep everyone aligned and motivated.

Figure 5.1

SMART GOALS WORKSHEET

GOAL	MY GOAL IS...	✓
Be specific and precise. Include the measure and time frame.	Specific	☐
	Measurable	☐
CHALLENGES	Attainable	☐
What are the challenges to overcome? What resources and skills are needed?	Relevant	☐
	Time-bound	☐
PURPOSE	COMPLETION DATE	
Why is the goal relevant? What are the benefits?		

KEY STEPS

How will you achieve your goal? What are the milestones and key steps?

Description	Start Date	Complete Date	✓
			☐
			☐
			☐
			☐
			☐
			☐

MEASURE

Keep a log of your progress

Date	Measure	Date	Measure	Date	Measure	Date	Measure

We have created a SMART goals worksheet to help you with this exercise (figure 5.1). You can download a copy from the resource page at www.YourFamilyYourFinances.com/Playbook-Resources.

Setting financial goals is an art that requires clarity, realism, and a keen understanding of your family's unique circumstances and aspirations. By effectively leveraging the SMART criteria, visualizing success, and prioritizing, your family can navigate the path to financial security and fulfillment with confidence and unity.

Remember, the journey to achieving your financial goals is as significant as the goals themselves, offering invaluable lessons and opportunities for growth along the way.

Creating a Plan to Achieve Goals

The first step in turning your financial goals from dreams into reality is aligning your family budget. This alignment ensures that your spending habits and saving efforts directly contribute to your goal achievement.

- **Allocate Funds Wisely:** Revisit your budget to identify areas where you can cut back on non-essential spending and redirect those funds toward your goals. This might mean sacrificing some wants in the short-term for significant long-term gains.

- **Flexibility is Key:** Life is unpredictable, and your budget should be too. Be prepared to adjust your budget as needed, whether in response to unexpected expenses or changes in income, and always keep your financial goals in sight.

The Power of Automating Your Savings

Automating your savings is like setting your financial goals on cruise control. By automatically transferring funds to savings or investment accounts designated for specific goals, you're ensuring consistent progress without the temptation to spend those funds elsewhere.

- **Direct Transfers:** Set up automatic transfers from your checking account to savings or investment accounts right after payday. This "pay yourself first" approach ensures your goals are prioritized.

- **Dedicated Accounts:** Consider having separate savings accounts for different goals. This segmentation makes it easier to track progress and keeps you motivated as you see each account grow.

Keeping Track: Monitoring and Adjusting Your Plan

Achieving financial goals is a dynamic process that requires regular monitoring and the willingness to adjust your plan as necessary.

Schedule monthly family meetings to review the progress toward your goals. These check-ins allow you to celebrate successes, identify challenges, and discuss any needed adjustments. Be ready to modify your goals or strategies in response to changes in your financial situation or priorities. If a goal becomes less relevant or achievable, shifting focus to more pressing objectives is okay.

Don't wait until you've reached a goal to celebrate. Acknowledge and reward your family's progress along the way. These celebrations can be simple and should reinforce the value of teamwork and perseverance.

Figure 5.2

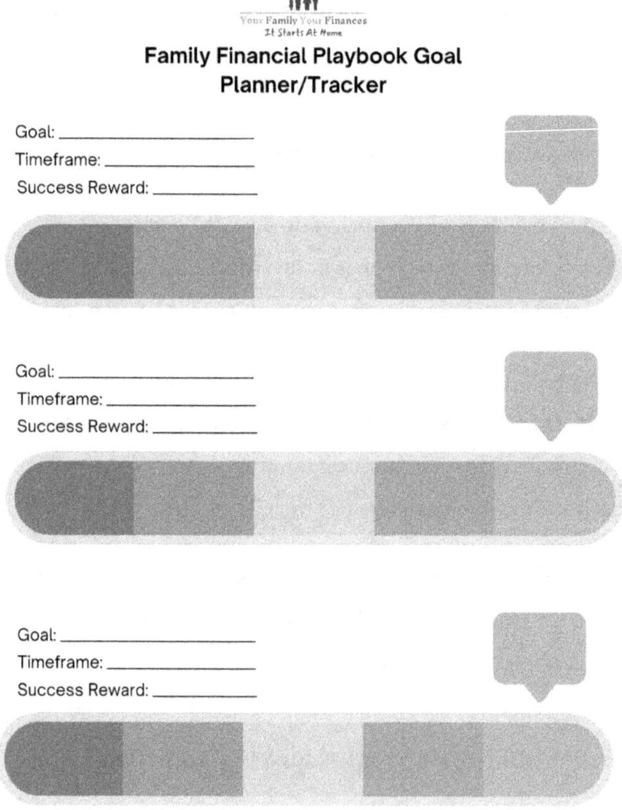

Figure 5.2 – To make it easier for you to track, we have created a Goal Process tracker for you to use. As with all the other tools in this book, you can download a copy through the resource page for the book at www.YourFamilyYourFinances.com/playbook-resources.

Creating and following a plan to achieve your financial goals involves more than just setting them; it requires aligning your budget, automating savings, and regularly monitoring your progress. By taking these steps, you and your family can confidently navigate the path to your financial aspirations, making adjustments as needed and celebrating your journey along the way.

Activity: Goal-Setting Workshop

Transforming financial aspirations into achievable goals is a critical step toward financial wellness for any family. This goal-setting workshop is designed to be a practical, interactive process that brings your family together to identify, refine, and plan for your financial future.

Step 1: Brainstorming Session

Gather your family in a comfortable space that's free from distractions. Equip yourselves with a whiteboard, flip chart, large sheets of paper, and plenty of markers or pens.

- **Open Discussion:** Encourage every family member to share their ideas for potential financial goals. At this stage, no idea is too big or small, from saving for a new video game to planning for college or retirement.

- **Capture Everything:** Write down all the suggestions. This inclusive approach ensures that everyone feels their voice is heard and valued.

Step 2: SMART Goal-Setting

With all potential goals laid out, it's time to refine them using the SMART framework, ensuring each goal is Specific, Measurable, Achievable, Relevant, and Time-bound.

- **Specific:** Clarify each goal to ensure it's well-defined. For example, "save for a family vacation to Hawaii" instead of "save for a trip."

- **Measurable:** Assign a dollar amount to each goal to make it trackable.

- **Achievable:** Ensure the goal is realistic, given your family's financial situation.

- **Relevant:** Confirm that the goal aligns with your family's values and long-term objectives.

- **Time-bound:** Set a deadline for achieving each goal to create urgency and focus.

Step 3: Action Plan Development

Develop a detailed action plan for each SMART goal. This plan will map out how you'll move from where you are now to where you want to be.

Specific Steps: Break down each goal into actionable steps. For example, suppose your goal is to save for a vacation. In that case, steps might include:

1. Setting a monthly saving target.

2. Cutting back on dining out.

3. Finding a side job for extra income.

Assign Responsibilities: Determine who in the family will be responsible for each plan part. Assigning roles plays to each member's strengths and interests, fostering engagement and accountability.

Timeline: Establish a timeframe for each plan step, creating mini-deadlines leading to the overall goal deadline.

Wrap-Up: Commitment and Celebration

Once you've developed action plans for each goal, have each family member verbally commit to their responsibilities. This formal commitment reinforces the importance of teamwork and individual contribution.

Conclude your workshop with a small celebration. This could be a special snack, a family game, or simply words of encouragement. Celebrating the completion of the planning process underscores the value of setting and working together to achieve goals.

This goal-setting workshop is not just about planning for the future; it's a valuable opportunity for your family to come together, share dreams, and commit to supporting each other. By taking these steps, you create a shared vision for your financial future and lay a practical roadmap to turn your family's financial goals into reality.

Case Study: The Nguyen Family's Goal-Setting Workshop

Meet the Nguyen family: Linh and Minh, with their daughters, Tessa (12) and Zoe (8). They are the ultimate immigrant story. Coming to the United States at the end of the Vietnam War, Linh and Minh's families settled in South Texas.

As a fisherman in Vietnam, Linh's father decided to start a small shrimp fishing business on the Texas Gulf Coast. When Linh took over the company, it grew to a fleet of five boats. It has since grown into one of the largest fleets on the Texas Coast. Lihn and Minh were high school sweethearts who married soon after graduating from the University of Texas.

The Nguyens were committed to teaching their children about financial responsibility and the importance of setting and achieving goals. They conducted a goal-setting workshop to align their family's aspirations and plan for the future.

Brainstorming Dreams and Goals

On a sunny Saturday afternoon, the Nguyens gathered in their living room with a whiteboard, colorful markers, and an open mind. The brainstorming session began with each family member sharing their dreams and financial goals, big and small. Tessa hoped to save for a laptop for college, while Zoe wished for a new bicycle. Linh and Minh wanted to start a college fund for the girls and save for a family vacation to Vietnam to explore their heritage.

Refining Goals with SMART Criteria

Once all ideas were on the board, the family used the SMART criteria to refine their goals. Tessa's laptop goal became, "Save $1,000 for a laptop by next summer," making it specific, measurable, achievable, relevant, and time-bound. Each goal was similarly defined, creating a clear roadmap for the family's financial journey.

Developing Action Plans

The Nguyens then worked together to develop action plans for each goal. They assigned responsibilities, such as Minh researching high-interest savings accounts for the college fund and Linh finding creative ways to cut back on monthly expenses. Tessa decided to take on extra babysitting jobs. Zoe offered to help with household chores for a small allowance to save for her bicycle.

Commitment and Celebration

With plans in place, each family member committed to their roles, understanding that achieving their goals would require teamwork and dedication. To celebrate the day's progress, the Nguyens ordered pizza. They watched their favorite movie, reinforcing the joy and unity in working towards common goals.

A Year of Progress

A year later, the Nguyens met their goals, with Tessa proudly purchasing her laptop and Zoe riding her new bike around the neighborhood. The college fund was well underway, and the family was planning their trip to Vietnam, excited about the adventure ahead. The goal-setting workshop brought them closer as a family. It taught valuable lessons about planning, saving, and working together towards a brighter future.

The Nguyen family's story exemplifies the power of collaborative goal-setting and its positive impact on a family's financial well-being and relationships. By engaging in a structured workshop to set and plan for their financial goals, the Nguyens turned their dreams into achievable milestones, fostering a sense of accomplishment and teamwork.

Conclusion: The Journey Towards Achieving Financial Goals

As we conclude this chapter on setting and achieving financial goals, it's essential to recognize you and your family's empowering journey. Goal-setting is more than just a financial exercise; it's a unifying activity that can significantly enhance your family's financial literacy, cohesion, and future prosperity.

Continuous Learning and Engagement

The journey of financial growth and goal achievement is ongoing, filled with opportunities for learning and engagement. To support you on this path:

- **YourFamilyYourFinances.com:** This resource hub provides tools, articles, and guidance to assist families in goal-setting and financial planning. From creating actionable plans to adjusting strategies to meet changing circumstances, the website is invaluable for families committed to financial success.

- ***Your Family Your Finances* Episodes (yfyf.YourHomeTV.com):** For those who appreciate learning through examples, select episodes of the *Your Family Your Finances* show delve into goal-setting and planning with real-life scenarios and expert advice. These episodes provide practical insights and motivation to keep your family inspired and on track.

The Power of Goals

Setting and working towards financial goals is an empowering process that does more than aim for material achievements. It is about how setting goals collectively strengthens family bonds, as each member contributes to and supports the family's financial well-being. Through setting goals, families learn to navigate financial challenges, make informed decisions, and adapt to changes in their financial landscape. Achieving financial goals sets the foundation for future success, creating a cycle of learning, growing, and accomplishing even greater aspirations.

Celebrate and Learn

Remember to celebrate each milestone on your journey. These celebrations reinforce the positive behaviors and teamwork that contributed to your success. Equally important is learning from every experience, using setbacks as stepping stones to greater understanding and resilience.

The path to achieving your family's financial goals may be challenging. Still, the rewards—financial security, enhanced relationships, and the fulfillment of dreams—are immeasurable. As you continue this journey, keep your goals in sight, remain adaptable, and draw strength from your family's collective commitment to success.

Here's to setting goals, embracing the journey, and building a prosperous future together. Your family's financial dreams are not just within reach—they're achievable, one goal at a time. Let's continue to learn, grow, and celebrate every step of the way.

In the next chapter, you will learn how to invest together as a family. This is a wonderful opportunity for parents to learn some things they probably didn't know and for kids to learn a skill that will help them grow their wealth early on in their lives.

Financial goals are the foundation for your family's financial plans. They are not just about numbers or milestones but are deeply intertwined with your family's aspirations, dreams, and quality of life.

Chapter 6

Investing As A Family

"Investing should be more like watching paint dry or watching grass grow. If you want excitement, take $800 and go to Las Vegas." - Paul Samuelson

Welcome to a journey that might seem daunting initially but is truly exciting—investing as a family. Investing is often shrouded in complexity and misconceptions, leading many to believe it's reserved for the financially savvy or the wealthy. However, this chapter aims to demystify investing, showcasing it as a crucial tool accessible to families at any financial stage seeking to secure and grow their wealth over time.

The Essence of Investing

At its core, investing involves allocating resources, usually money, to generate an income or profit. It's about putting your money to work so it can grow over the years, contributing to your family's financial security and long-term aspirations. Whether buying stocks, bonds, mutual funds, or investing in real estate, the goal is the same: to increase your financial resources.

Why Invest?

There needs to be more than the simple act of saving money in a traditional savings account to grow your wealth significantly, especially considering inflation's impact on purchasing power. Investing, however, offers the potential for higher returns, making it a critical component of any robust financial plan. In this chapter, we will begin with the basics of the power of compound interest and get into the components of the markets that you can invest in. You will gain a basic knowledge of investing in this book. Our next book in the series *The Family Investment Playbook* focuses more on the investment process. Let's get started by looking at compound interest.

The Power of Compound Interest

One of the most compelling reasons to start investing is the power of compound interest. Albert Einstein famously called compound interest the eighth wonder of the world, stating, "He who understands it, earns it; he who doesn't, pays it." Compound interest allows your investments to grow exponentially over time, as the returns you earn each year are reinvested to generate their returns.

Figure 6.1 – Power of Compounding

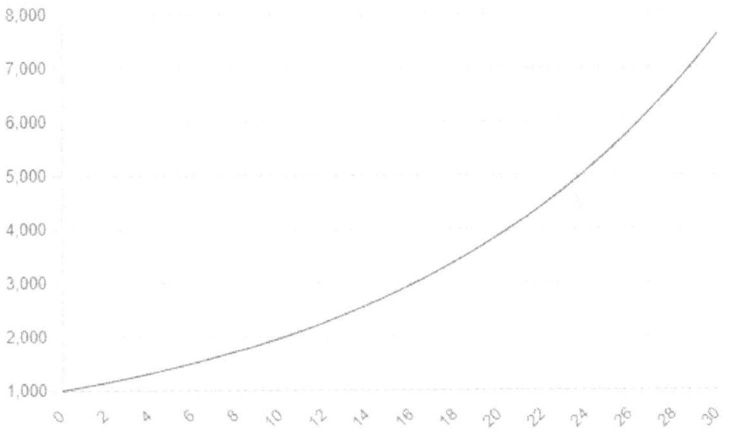

Figure 6.1 – illustrates the power of compounding. This example starts with $1000 and compounding over the next 30 years at 7% interest.

For parents, here are some discussion points to share with your children:

- Starting Amount: $1000

- Compound Growth Rate: 7% per year

- No additional investments were made

- ○ After 10 years: The investment grows to $1967.15

- ○ After 20 years: The investment grows to $3869.68

- ○ After 30 years: The investment grows to $7612.26

Discussion Points:

- **Early Start**: Highlight the importance of starting to save early. The longer the money is invested, the more it grows due to compound interest.

- **Growth Over Time**: Show how the investment more than doubles every 10 years, illustrating the exponential growth effect of compounding.

- **Financial Goals**: Encourage children to set financial goals and understand how saving and investing can help achieve those goals over time.

If you would like to play with different scenarios, including adding more money over time, I recommend one of my favorite sites for online financial calculators: Dinkytown.net. This calculator can calculate future value: https://www.dinkytown.net/java/future-value-calculator.html.

Investing as a Family

Investing as a family isn't just about growing your wealth; it's also about education and shared goals. It presents an opportunity to teach children about money, investment principles, and the value of long-term planning. By involving the whole family, you can make financial decisions reflecting your collective values and goals, investing in a shared journey toward financial freedom and security.

By starting this chapter with an engaging and clear introduction to investing, we aim to encourage families to see investing, not as a daunting task reserved for the few, but as an accessible and vital part of achieving financial stability and realizing their long-term dreams. Through investing, families can harness the potential to grow their wealth, ensuring a brighter economic future for themselves and future generations.

Why Start Investing Early?

One of the most compelling reasons to start investing early is the time value of money. This principle suggests that a dollar in hand today is worth more than a dollar received in the future because of its potential earning capacity. The earlier you invest, the more time your money has to grow through the magic of compound interest.

Imagine planting a tree. The sooner you plant it, the longer it will grow, mature, and bear fruit. Similarly, investing money grows over time, and the earnings on your initial investment begin to earn their own returns.

This cycle continues, potentially increasing your wealth at an accelerating rate. Starting to invest early can mean the difference between a modest nest egg and a substantial financial legacy for families.

Educational Value

Beyond the financial benefits, involving your children in investment decisions from an early age provides invaluable learning opportunities. It opens up conversations about money, savings, and the broader economy, helping them understand the importance of financial planning and the role of various investment vehicles.As children watch their investments grow, they learn firsthand about the stock market, interest rates, and economic factors that affect their savings. This real-world education is something they're likely to miss in school.

Participating in family investment decisions teaches children the value of saving and the discipline required for long-term financial success. They also understand that instant gratification can be traded for significant future gains. Engaging with investments can also spark an entrepreneurial spirit in young family members. It encourages them to consider how businesses grow, adapt, and succeed in a competitive environment.

Figure 6.1

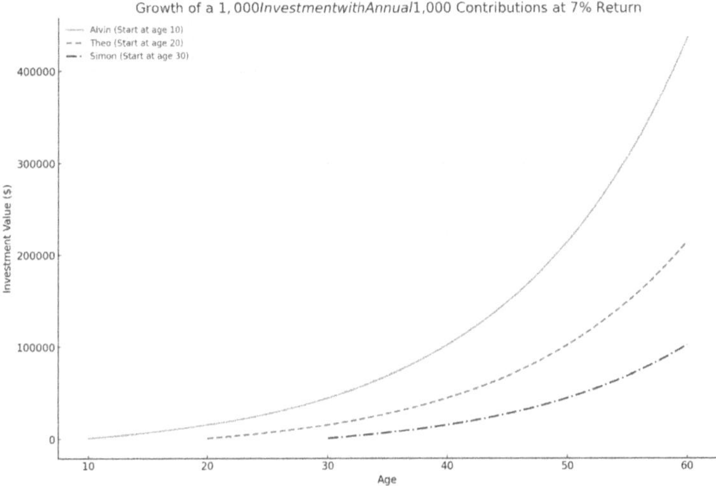

Figure 6.2 illustrates the growth of an initial investment of $https://prod.content.atticus.io /images/growthlkwb7NWPdVyd_ce.png1,000 with an additional annual contribution of $1,000 at a 7% annual return for three individuals starting at different ages: Alvin at 10, Theo at 20, and Simon at 30, tracked up until the age of 60. Each line begins at the respective start age of the individual, accurately reflecting the scenario for Alvin, Theo, and Simon.

So that children understand the benefits of starting early, let's look at a scenario similar to that in Figure 6.1. However, this time, we will look at three investors starting at different times. In Figure 6.2, we look at three hypothetical investors: Alvin, Theo, and Simon. They start at ages 10, 20, and 30, each investing the same amount ($1000) and at the same investment rate (7%). This representation effectively demonstrates the compounded effect of both early investing and the impact of consistent annual contributions. The lines for Alvin, Theo, and Simon distinctly show how the combination of time and additional investments can dramatically increase the final investment value, with Alvin's starting the earliest and thus achieving the highest growth by age.

Understanding the significance of starting investments early cannot be overstated. The combined power of the time value of money and compound interest can significantly impact wealth accumulation, providing a secure financial future. Moreover, the process offers rich educational value, equipping the next generation with essential knowledge and skills for making wise financial decisions. By embedding these principles early on, families can set the stage for lasting financial health and success.

Types of Investing for Families

Investing can seem complex, but at its heart, it's about choosing where to put your money to work for you and your family's future. Let's break down two fundamental investment types: stocks and bonds.

When you buy stocks, you're purchasing a small piece of ownership in a company. If the company does well, the value of your stock can grow, and you may receive dividends as your share of the profits. Think of it like buying a tiny slice of a big pie; as the pie grows, so does the value of your slice.

Buying a bond means lending money to an entity (like the government or a corporation) for a period. In return, they agree to pay you the principal amount plus interest at predetermined intervals. It's akin to giving a loan and then getting your money back with interest.

Mutual Funds and ETFs: Pooling Resources for Diversification

For families looking to diversify their investments without taking on too much risk, mutual funds and ETFs (Exchange-Traded Funds) offer an attractive solution. Mutual Funds are pools of money collected from many investors to invest in a diversified portfolio of stocks, bonds, or other assets. It's like joining a group where everyone chips in to buy a bigger, varied collection of investments managed by a professional.

Similar to mutual funds, ETFs pool investments but are traded on stock exchanges like individual stocks. This means you can buy and sell shares of ETFs throughout the trading day at market price. They offer the diversification of mutual funds with the flexibility of stocks.

Saving for College: Investing in Education

Many families' major financial goal is saving for their children's education. Specific investment accounts like 529 plans can be instrumental in achieving this goal. Educational investing does not have to be only for college. 529 plans can be used for any post-secondary education, such as trade schools, community college programs, and even some certification programs.

These tax-advantaged savings plans are designed to encourage saving for future education costs. Contributions grow tax-free, and withdrawals used for qualified education expenses are not taxed. Think of it as a special savings account where the government gives you tax breaks as a reward for saving for education.

Opening a 529 plan is relatively straightforward. You can choose a plan offered by your state or any other state that allows non-resident enrollees. Consider the investment options, fees, and whether your state offers any tax benefits for contributions.

While 529s can be one of the most tax-efficient strategies for college, they are not the only way. Another strategy is to set up a UTMA (Uniform Trust to Minors Account), where you can control and invest in different investments, such as real estate and insurance. In our practice, we use a specialized insurance strategy that can be used to fund college and later supplement retirement.

Finding a qualified professional, such as a Certified College Funding Specialist (CCFS) through www.hireaccfs.com, can be an excellent resource.

Retirement Accounts

One of the most common goals we all have is retirement. This goal affects not only parents but also kids. Learning together can help the entire family. Let's break down some essentials about retirement investment accounts like 401(k)s, IRAs, and growth annuities. These are like the superheroes of the investment world, each with their own special powers to help you save for those golden years.

1. **401(k)s: Your Work-Based Super Saver:** Imagine you've got a piggy bank at work where a slice of your paycheck goes in before taxes even get a whiff of it. That's your 401(k). It's like a secret tunnel where your money escapes taxes and grows, tax-deferred, until you're ready to retire. Plus, some employers will match what you put, up to a certain percentage (free money alert!). The catch? There's a limit to how much you can contribute each year, and there are rules about when you can take the money out without penalties. But it's a powerful way to build up that retirement fund.

2. **IRAs: The Personal Touch to Retirement Saving:** IRAs, or Individual Retirement Accounts, are personal savings for retirement that you set up on your own. There are two main types: traditional and Roth. With a Traditional IRA, you can now deduct your contributions on your taxes, and the money grows tax-deferred. A Roth IRA flips the script—you pay taxes on what you put in now, but when it's time to withdraw, it's all yours, tax-free.

3. **Growth Annuities: The Long Game Player:** Here's where it gets a bit more "grown-up." Annuities are contracts with an insurance company. You give them a lump sum or make payments over time, and they promise to pay you back with interest later on, usually when you retire. Growth annuities focus on—you guessed it—growth, aiming to increase your investment over time, before you start getting payments. They can be a bit complex and come with fees and terms you need to understand, but they're another tool in the retirement savings tool belt. One of the best parts is that there is virtually no limit on their contribution amount.

Why Bother with These?

Think of retirement accounts as the VIP section of investing. They come with tax perks that help your money grow more efficiently over time. By diversifying where you save for retirement—not just *how* you invest—you can create a solid foundation that supports you when you're older and ready to enjoy life without punching the clock. Remember, the goal here isn't just to save money; it's to invest in your future self. So, get to know these accounts while you're young (or young-ish). Talk to a financial advisor if you can. Make informed choices about where to stash your retirement savings, and set yourself up for a smoother, more relaxed ride into your sunset years.

With these expanded insights into types of retirement investment accounts, you're better equipped to make choices that suit your long-term financial goals and lifestyle aspirations. Let's make those golden years as golden as possible!

Understanding the various available investments and the appropriate accounts is crucial for families navigating the path to financial security and growth. From the direct ownership of stocks to the lending model of bonds and the diversified approach of mutual funds and ETFs, there are options to suit different risk tolerances and goals. Moreover, investing in a 529 plan offers a focused way to address the significant goal of funding education, combining the benefits of investing with tax advantages.

Finally, the tax advantages of the different retirement accounts can help you save on taxes now or in the future. By exploring these options, families can make informed decisions that align with their aspirations and financial plans.

Creating an Investment Plan

An effective investment plan is the backbone of successful financial growth for any family. It's about more than just choosing where to put your money; it's a comprehensive approach that aligns with your family's financial objectives, risk tolerance, and future aspirations. Let's explore creating an investment plan that works for your family.

Goal Setting: The Foundation of Your Investment Plan

As discussed in Chapter 6, the first step in creating an investment plan is establishing clear, achievable goals. These goals should reflect what you're investing in for retirement, your children's education, a family home, or financial security. Instead of a vague goal like "save for the future," define what that future looks like. How much will you need? When will you need it? Just like our exercises in the goal planning section, we also need to use SMART goals here. Assign a timeframe to each goal. Knowing whether a goal is short-term, medium-term, or long-term can help you select the appropriate investment vehicles.

Risk Assessment: Understanding Your Family's Comfort Level

Every investment has its own set of risks and potential rewards. Understanding your family's risk tolerance is crucial to creating a plan that aligns with your comfort level.

Many online platforms offer questionnaires designed to help you gauge your risk tolerance. These can be a great starting point for understanding how much investment risk you're willing to take. Forbes magazine published an article on this (https://www.forbes.com/advisor/investing/investment-risk-tolerance-quiz/), which should be a good starting point for you and your family. For the young ones, this may be a bit above their heads because they think in dollars and cents, whereas adults tend to think in thousands of dollars.

Once you understand your risk tolerance, it is time to make some investment decisions. Once you know your risk tolerance, choose investments that fit. For example, stocks may be suitable for families comfortable with higher risk for potentially higher returns. At the same time, bonds may be better for those seeking more stability.

What is your contribution style going to be?

One of the most powerful aspects of investing is the potential for compound growth, which requires consistent contributions over time.

- **Automate Contributions:** Like saving, automating your investment contributions can ensure you regularly add to your investments without thinking about it each month.

- **Start Small:** Even small amounts can grow significantly over time, thanks to compound interest. Take your time investing large sums; start with what you can afford now.

Figure 6.2

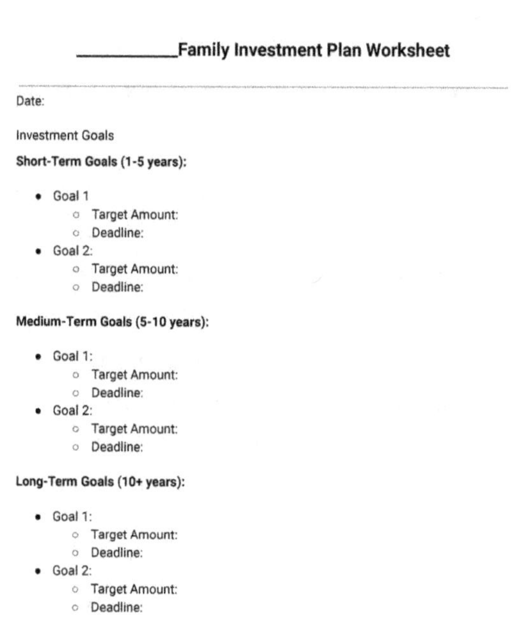

___________Family Investment Plan Worksheet

Date:

Investment Goals

Short-Term Goals (1-5 years):

- Goal 1
  - Target Amount:
  - Deadline:
- Goal 2:
  - Target Amount:
  - Deadline:

Medium-Term Goals (5-10 years):

- Goal 1:
  - Target Amount:
  - Deadline:
- Goal 2:
  - Target Amount:
  - Deadline:

Long-Term Goals (10+ years):

- Goal 1:
  - Target Amount:
  - Deadline:
- Goal 2:
  - Target Amount:
  - Deadline:

Copyright 2024 - CPTX Media LLC

Figure 6.2 gives you an example of the Family Investment Plan Worksheet, which you can download from our website at www.YourFamilyYourFinances.com/playbook-resources.

An investment plan is essential for families looking to grow their wealth and achieve their financial goals. By setting clear objectives, understanding risk tolerance, and committing to regular contributions, families can confidently navigate the complexities of investing. Remember, investing aims to accumulate wealth and secure a financial future that aligns with your family's dreams and aspirations.

Activity: Family Investment Project

Engaging in a family investment project can be an enlightening experience, offering hands-on learning about the stock market and investment principles. It's a fantastic way to bring financial concepts to life, fostering teamwork and financial literacy among all family members. Here's how to embark on this educational journey together:

Step 1: Research Together

Begin by gathering as a family to research potential investments. This step is crucial in understanding the vast landscape of investment options, from stocks and mutual funds to ETFs.

- **Educational Resources:** Utilize financial news websites, investment platforms, and educational YouTube channels focused on investing in learning about different companies, mutual funds, and ETFs.

- **Understand Market Trends:** Introduce basic concepts of market trends and how they can affect investment performance. Discuss the importance of long-term investment strategies overreacting to short-term market fluctuations.

Step 2: Decision Making

After researching, it's time to decide which stock, mutual fund, or ETF you will follow as a family. This decision-making process is an excellent opportunity for everyone to voice their opinions and learnings.

- **Family Meeting:** Hold a family meeting to discuss potential investment choices. Encourage each family member to present an exciting investment and explain why it could be a good option.

- **Consider Diversification:** Discuss the concept of diversification and how choosing different types of investments can reduce risk. It's an essential principle in making informed investment decisions.

Step 3: Tracking Progress

Once you've chosen an investment to follow, please set up a system to track its performance over time. This ongoing activity turns your investment choice into a living project, offering continuous learning opportunities.

- **Template for Tracking:** Create a simple spreadsheet or use investment tracking apps to monitor the performance of your chosen investment. Include columns for the date, investment value, and relevant news or market changes.

- **Regular Check-ins:** Schedule monthly family meetings to review the investment's progress. Discuss what may have caused any changes in value, whether it's performing as expected, and what you can learn from it.

Figure 6.3

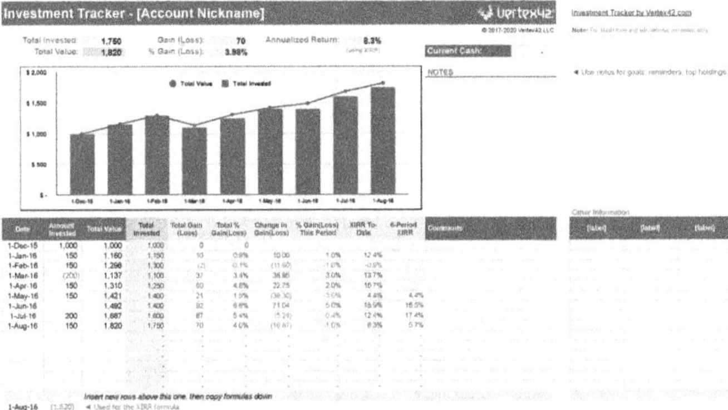

Figure 6.3 is a tracking spreadsheet to help you and your family track your investments. This one comes from our friends at Vertex42 (www.vertex42.com). This website has some of the best free Excel and Google Sheets templates available online. We have a copy of this spreadsheet available on the companion website for the book www.yourfamilyyourfinances.com/playbook-resources.

This family investment project is not just about potentially growing wealth; it's a powerful educational tool. Families can deepen their understanding of financial markets, investment strategies, and the economic factors that influence performance by researching, deciding on, and tracking an investment together. This project fosters communication, critical thinking, and a collaborative approach to financial decision-making, laying the groundwork for informed and savvy investors in the family.

Case Study: The Harper Family's Investment Adventure

Meet the Harper family: Jenna and Alex, with their teenagers, Marcus and Eliza. While Alex and Jenna have 401k plans through their jobs, they don't understand what they are investing in. Having grown up in families that did not talk about investments or money, they decided that they wanted to know more about investing and wanted to get Marcus and Eliza involved in learning alongside their parents.

The Harpers decided to expand their financial knowledge. They embarked on a family investment project to learn firsthand about the stock market and investment principles.

Embarking on the Research Journey

The project started with a family meeting, where Jenna introduced the idea. They all agreed to dedicate the next month to learning about investments and selecting one stock, mutual fund, or ETF to track. They divided the research tasks according to interest: Jenna focused on mutual funds, Alex on ETFs, and the kids on individual stocks, particularly those related to technology and environmental sustainability, areas they were passionate about.

Each family member utilized different resources for research. Marcus and Eliza enjoyed educational YouTube channels and podcasts on investing for beginners. At the same time, Jenna and Alex preferred reading financial news websites and investment analysis reports.

Making the Decision

After weeks of research and lively dinner table discussions about potential investments, the Harpers held a decision-making meeting. Each presented their findings, including possible risks and benefits. Marcus was particularly persuasive about a clean energy ETF that aligned with the family's values of sustainability and showed promising growth potential.

After a thoughtful discussion, they decided to "invest" in the clean energy ETF Marcus suggested. They used a stock market simulation app to invest virtual money, planning to track its performance as if it were a real investment.

Tracking and Learning

Alex created a simple spreadsheet for the family to log the ETF's performance weekly. They included news headlines that could impact the stock market to understand the correlation between market trends and their investment's value.

Monthly family meetings became an exciting event where they reviewed the ETF's performance, celebrated when it was up, and discussed strategies for managing downturns. These sessions became invaluable lessons in market dynamics, investment patience, and the importance of diversification.

Reflections on the Investment Adventure

After six months, the Harpers concluded their project. While their virtual investment had ups and downs, the knowledge and experience gained were profoundly positive. Marcus and Eliza developed a keen interest in sustainable investing. Jenna planned to start her actual investment portfolio, and Alex became an advocate for financial literacy in his community.

The Harper's investment adventure was more than just a project; it was a transformative experience that enhanced their financial literacy, brought them closer as a family, and sparked new interests and future goals. It demonstrated that with curiosity, collaboration, and a willingness to learn, investing can be an accessible and rewarding journey for any family.

Through the Harper family's journey, this case study showcases the educational and bonding potential of embarking on a family investment project. Their experience underscores that investing is a pathway to financial growth and a valuable tool for learning, engagement, and shared discovery.

Wrap-Up: Embracing the Investment Journey Together

As we conclude this chapter on investing as a family, it's clear that the journey into the world of investments is both enriching and enlightening. Investing isn't solely about the potential financial returns; it's about embarking on a path of learning, growth, and shared experiences that can bring your family closer and set the foundation for a prosperous future.

Investing as a family is more than a financial endeavor; it's a journey that fosters patience, teaches risk management, and highlights the rewards of strategic, long-term planning. It's an opportunity to:

- **Build a Legacy:** Through shared investment goals and strategies, you're building wealth and creating a legacy of financial savvy and stability that can benefit future generations.

- **Teach Valuable Life Lessons:** The investment journey is ripe with lessons on the importance of research, patience, and adapting to change—invaluable lessons in finances and life.

- **Strengthen Family Bonds:** Collaborating on investment decisions and celebrating milestones reinforces family unity and shared purpose, turning individual aspirations into collective achievements.

Looking Ahead

As you and your family continue to explore and engage with the world of investing, remember that each step, whether a success or a learning experience, is valuable. Embrace the journey with an open mind and a spirit of collaboration. The world of investing offers a unique opportunity to grow not just your family's wealth but also your knowledge, experiences, and bonds with each other.

Investing is a journey best undertaken together, where the shared goals and experiences become as rewarding as the financial gains. Here's to your family's investment journey—discovery, growth, and shared success. Let this be an exciting adventure that enriches your family's present and future, teaching invaluable lessons and building a lasting legacy.

As we move into the next chapter, we will discuss how to handle your finances when things don't go as expected.

Make a Difference with Your Review

"No one has ever become poor by giving." - Anne Frank

Unlock the Power of Generosity

Hey there! Did you know that people who give without expecting anything in return live longer, happier lives and often make more money? Pretty cool, right? So, let's try to make that magic happen together!

I have a question for you...

Would you help someone you've never met, even if you never got credit for it?

Who is this person, you ask? They are just like you. Or, at least, like you used to be. They want to understand money, make good choices, and help their family, but they're unsure where to start.

My mission with "The Family Finance Playbook" is to make financial literacy easy and fun for everyone. The only way to do that is to reach everyone.

This is where you come in. Most people judge a book by its cover (and its reviews). So, here's my ask on behalf of a family you've never met:

Please help that family by leaving a review for this book.

Your review costs no money and takes less than 60 seconds, but it could change another family's life forever. Your review could help...

- ...one more family to understand how to save for the future.

- ...one more teen learn the importance of budgeting.

- ...one more parent teach their kids about money.

- ...one more person feel confident about their financial choices.

- ...one more dream come true.

To get that 'feel good' feeling and help someone for real, all you have to do is leave a review.

Simply scan the QR code below to leave your review:

https://www.amazon.com/review/review-your-purchases/?asin=B0DBRBF4K4

If you feel good about helping another family, you are my kind of person. Welcome to the club. You're one of us.

I'm so excited to help you and your family achieve your financial goals. The tips and tricks in the coming chapters will be great.

Thank you from the bottom of my heart. Now, back to our regularly scheduled program.

Your biggest fan,

Jeff Kikel

PS—Fun fact: Helping someone else makes you feel great, too! If you think this book could help a friend, send it their way.

At its core, investing involves allocating resources, usually money, to generate an income or profit. It's about putting your money to work so it can grow over the years, contributing to your family's financial security and long-term aspirations

Chapter 7

Preparing For The Unexpected

"Life's greatest adventures lie in the unexpected twists and turns. It's not about controlling the storm, but learning to dance in the rain."
– Jeff Kikel

In life's journey, the unexpected is the only certainty. Whether a minor hiccup or a significant emergency, unforeseen events can disrupt even the most carefully laid financial plans. This chapter focuses on the critical importance of financial preparedness, offering strategies and insights to help your family navigate the unpredictable with confidence and resilience.

The Reality of Unforeseen Expenses

No family is immune to life's surprises—sudden car repairs, unexpected medical bills, or even job loss. These events can vary in scale but share a common trait: they're rarely planned for, and their timing can be inconvenient at best and devastating at worst.

The impact of such surprises on a family's financial stability can be significant. These unexpected expenses can lead to debt, stress, and a cascade of financial challenges without adequate preparation. However, with proactive planning and a solid emergency fund, families can weather these storms with far less turmoil.

The Value of Proactive Planning

Proactive financial planning is about avoiding negative outcomes and creating a buffer that allows your family to face challenges without derailing your long-term financial goals. This planning involves:

- **Building an Emergency Fund:** As previously mentioned in our discussions on saving, an emergency fund is a cornerstone of financial preparedness. It's a dedicated pool of resources designed to cover unexpected expenses without the need to dip into savings earmarked for other goals.

- **Insurance:** Appropriate insurance coverage, from health to home and auto, is pivotal in mitigating financial risk. It ensures you're protected against potentially overwhelming costs when the unforeseen strikes.

- **Flexible Financial Planning:** A resilient financial plan can adapt to changes. This flexibility means regularly reviewing and adjusting your budget, savings, and investment strategies for new realities.

Embracing financial preparedness equips your family to handle life's uncertainties with grace. It's about acknowledging the potential for unexpected events and taking steps to mitigate their impact. This chapter will guide you through establishing a robust emergency fund, securing appropriate insurance coverage, and fostering a flexible approach to financial planning, ensuring that your family is ready for whatever lies ahead. By prioritizing preparedness, you safeguard your finances, peace of mind, and family's well-being.

Building an Emergency Fund

An emergency fund acts as your family's financial safety net, designed to catch you during life's unexpected falls. It's a dedicated stash of money set aside specifically for unforeseen expenses—those not accounted for in your regular budgeting. This could range from sudden car repairs to unexpected medical bills or job loss. The primary role of an emergency fund is to provide a buffer that allows you to handle these surprises without resorting to debt or dipping into savings meant for other purposes.

How Much to Save

Determining the right amount for your emergency fund can vary based on your family's circumstances. Still, there are general guidelines to help you set a target:

- **Start Small:** Initially, aim for a fund of $1,000. This amount can cover many minor emergencies, offering security as you build towards a larger fund.

- **Cover 3-6 Months of Expenses:** The ultimate goal is to have enough in your emergency fund to cover 3-6 months of living expenses. This provides substantial protection in case of significant financial disruptions, like a job loss. Calculating your monthly expenses and multiplying that by the number of months will give you your target amount.

Strategies for Building the Fund

Creating and growing an emergency fund takes time and dedication. Here are practical strategies to help you build your fund gradually:

- **Fixed Percentage of Income:** One of the simplest ways to build your emergency fund is to allocate a fixed monthly income. Whether it's 5%, 10%, or more, make this contribution as regular as paying a bill.

- **Windfalls and Unexpected Income:** Any unexpected income—tax refunds, bonuses, or gifts—can be a boon to your emergency fund. Allocating a portion or the entirety of these windfalls to your emergency fund can significantly accelerate your progress.

- **Cut Back on Non-Essentials:** Review your budget for areas where you can reduce non-essential spending. Redirecting even small amounts from discretionary expenses to your emergency fund can make a difference over time.

- **Automate Your Savings:** Set up an automatic transfer from your checking account to your emergency fund. Automating this process makes it easier to stay consistent and prevents the temptation to spend those funds elsewhere.

Building an emergency fund is an essential step in preparing for the unexpected. By starting small, setting clear goals, and employing strategic saving methods, families can establish a financial safety net that protects against life's uncertainties. This fund safeguards your financial stability and provides peace of mind, knowing you're prepared to face challenges without compromising your financial future.

Insurance: Understanding and Choosing the Right Policies

Insurance acts as a critical layer of protection in financial preparedness. It's designed to safeguard you and your family from significant financial losses due to unforeseen events. Let's explore the key types of insurance that form the pillars of a comprehensive financial plan:

- **Health Insurance:** Covers medical expenses resulting from illnesses or injuries. Protecting against high healthcare costs and ensuring access to necessary medical care is essential.

- **Life Insurance:** Provides financial support to beneficiaries (usually family members) in the event of the policyholder's death. Families with dependents must ensure financial stability during difficult times.

- **Homeowner's/Renter's Insurance:** Protects your home and possessions from damage or theft. Homeowner's insurance is necessary for property owners, while renter's insurance covers those who lease their living spaces.

- **Auto Insurance:** Covers costs associated with car accidents, including vehicle repairs and medical expenses. It's required by law in most places and vital for anyone who owns or operates a vehicle.

- **Disability Insurance:** Offers income protection if you cannot work due to a disability. It's an important consideration for ensuring continued financial support in case of long-term illness or injury.

Choosing the Right Coverage

Selecting the right insurance policies involves assessing your family's unique needs, understanding available options, and making informed decisions about coverage levels. Here are some tips to guide you through this process:

- **Assess Your Family's Needs:** Consider your family's specific circumstances, including dependents, assets, and potential risks. For example, if you're the primary breadwinner, life and disability insurance becomes particularly important.

- **Compare Policies:** Don't settle for the first policy you come across. Shop around and compare policies from different insurers to find the best coverage at the most reasonable price.

- **Understand Coverage Levels:** Closely to each policy's coverage and exclusions. Ensure the coverage levels are adequate to protect against significant financial loss without overpaying for unnecessary coverage.

- **Read the Fine Print:** Insurance policies can be complex. Take the time to read the details, and don't hesitate to ask questions or seek clarification from the insurer or a financial advisor.

- **Regular Reviews:** Your insurance needs may change over time due to life events such as marriage, childbirth, or purchasing a home. Review and adjust your coverage regularly to align with your family's needs.

Understanding and selecting the right insurance policies are crucial to preparing for the unexpected. Ensuring adequate coverage across different areas of your life protects your family from potentially devastating financial impacts. Insurance is not just about mitigating risks; it's an investment in your family's financial security and peace of mind. This is a place that I encourage you to work with a professional. I have sold insurance for over 25 years, but my expertise is in the area of life insurance and disability. Even with my experience, I work with an independent agent for my property and casualty insurance for my personal and business insurance. For the benefits and long-term savings strategies that we use for my team members, I work with a specialized team of agents who also work with my clients. The point I am making is no matter how much you know or how much experience you have, it is still important to have a team to advise you.

Creating a Financial Emergency Plan

Preparation begins with identification. The first step in crafting a financial emergency plan is recognizing potential risks that could impact your family's financial stability. These risks can vary widely depending on personal circumstances, including employment security, health issues, or regional concerns such as natural disasters.

When it comes to personal emergencies, there are several things that you need to consider. Consider job stability, potential health risks, or any family-specific factors affecting your financial situation. Also, be aware of broader risks, such as economic downturns or environmental factors that could indirectly impact your finances.

Developing a Response Strategy

Once you've identified potential risks, the next step is to devise a plan for managing your finances should those risks become a reality. A well-thought-out strategy can provide a roadmap for effectively navigating financial challenges.

- **Emergency Fund:** Reinforce the importance of your emergency fund as a financial buffer. Ensure it's adequately funded to cover expenses related to the identified risks.

- **Insurance Coverage:** Verify that your insurance policies provide adequate coverage for risks like medical emergencies, job loss (via disability insurance), and property damage.

- **Financial Prioritization:** Determine which expenses are non-negotiable and which can be reduced or eliminated in a crisis. This prioritization ensures that you can stretch your emergency fund further if needed.

- **Alternative Income Sources:** Identify alternative income sources or skills that could be leveraged in case of job loss. This could include freelance work, part-time jobs, or other side hustles.

Regular Review and Update

Change is the only constant in life; your financial emergency plan should reflect this reality. As your family grows and evolves, so should your approach to managing potential financial crises. Make it a habit to review your emergency plan at least once a year or after any significant life change (e.g., a new job, the birth of a child, moving houses). This plan should always be written down and not just in your head. Be prepared to adjust your plan based on changes in your financial situation, goals, or the external environment. This might include increasing your emergency fund target, updating insurance coverage, or reassessing potential risks.

When appropriate, include all family members in these reviews. This ensures everyone is informed and on the same page and fosters a sense of shared responsibility for the family's financial well-being.

Figure 7.1

Family Emergency Planning Checklist

Identifying Risks

☐ **Assess Environmental Risks:** Consider natural disasters common to your area (floods, hurricanes, earthquakes, etc.).
☐ **Evaluate Health Risks:** Consider any family health issues that could lead to emergencies.
☐ **Financial Vulnerabilities:** Identify potential financial crises, like job loss or unexpected major expenses.
☐ **Home Safety Check:** Review home security and safety to prevent or prepare for emergencies like fires or break-ins.

Developing a Response Strategy

☐ **Emergency Fund:** Aim to save at least 3-6 months' worth of living expenses.
☐ **Insurance Coverage:** Ensure adequate coverage for health, home, and vehicles. Consider life and disability insurance as well.
☐ **Healthcare Plan:** Have a list of emergency contacts, medical records, and healthcare proxies easily accessible.
☐ **Emergency Contacts List:** Compile a list of essential contacts, including family, friends, doctors, and local emergency services.
☐ **Evacuation Plan:** Create and practice an evacuation plan for natural disasters. Know your local evacuation routes and shelters.
☐ **Home Safety Kit:** Assemble an emergency kit with food, water, first aid, medications, flashlights, and other essentials.
☐ **Financial Documents:** Secure and make copies of important financial documents (bank accounts, deeds, insurance policies).
☐ Communication Plan: Decide on a family meeting point and a communication plan if separated during an emergency.

Conducting Regular Reviews

Creating a financial emergency plan is essential in safeguarding your family's future against the unknown. You can build a robust defense that minimizes financial disruption and fosters resilience by identifying potential risks, crafting a thoughtful response strategy, and committing to regular reviews and updates. Remember, the goal is not just to survive unexpected challenges but to emerge from them with your financial goals and family unity intact.

Like other tools in this book, you can access our Family Emergency Planning Checklist (figure 7.1) at www.yourfamilyyourfinances.com/playbook-resources.

Activity: Emergency Fund Challenge

A robust emergency fund is a cornerstone of financial preparedness. To kickstart or bolster this critical savings effort, we present the Emergency Fund Challenge—a fun and engaging way for your family to strengthen its financial safety net together.

Challenge Structure

The Emergency Fund Challenge is designed with clear, achievable milestones to build your savings systematically. Here's a suggested structure to get you started:

1. **First goal—$100:** Aim to save your first $100 within one month. This is the initial step that demonstrates commitment and begins building your fund.

2. **Second goal—$500:** Once you've hit the first milestone, expand your target to $500. Set a three-month timeline for this goal to build upon your initial success.

3. **Third goal—$1,000:** The final milestone of the challenge is reaching $1,000 in savings. Aim to accomplish this within the next six months, establishing a solid foundation for your emergency fund.

Family Participation

Encouraging contributions from all family members accelerate the growth of your emergency fund and reinforce the value of teamwork and collective financial responsibility.

- **Small Contributions Count:** Whether it's saving a portion of allowance money, contributing a fraction of a paycheck, or depositing unexpected windfalls, every contribution helps. Emphasize that it's not the amount that matters but the act of contributing itself.

- **Creative Saving Ideas:** Encourage family members to devise creative ways to save or earn extra money. These could include a garage sale, homemade crafts, or even a lemonade stand.

Reward System

Establish a reward system for reaching each milestone to keep motivation high and celebrate your family's progress. Opt for non-monetary rewards that emphasize togetherness and shared experiences.

- **First Milestone Reward:** Celebrate your first $100 with a family movie night at home. Let the kids pick the film and enjoy homemade popcorn together.

- **Second Milestone Reward:** Upon reaching $500, have a family game night. Bring out board games, card games, or video games everyone can enjoy.

- **Third Milestone Reward:** Hitting the $1,000 mark deserves a special celebration. Plan a family picnic in your favorite local park, bringing homemade treats and enjoying outdoor activities together.

The Emergency Fund Challenge is more than just a savings exercise; it's a family bonding activity that instills the principles of financial preparedness and the importance of working together toward common goals. By setting clear milestones, encouraging participation from all family members, and celebrating achievements with meaningful rewards, you can make building an emergency fund an enjoyable and rewarding experience for the whole family.

Case Study: The Rivera Family's Emergency Fund Evolution

Meet Carmen Rivera, a single mom navigating the complexities of raising three children: Maria (16), Juan (12), and little Sofia (7). While Carmen had always been meticulous with budgeting for daily expenses and future needs, the concept of an emergency fund had taken a backseat in the family's financial planning. Realizing the importance of being prepared for unexpected financial challenges, Carmen introduced the Emergency Fund Challenge to the family.

Launching the Challenge

One evening, Carmen gathered Maria, Juan, and Sofia to discuss building an emergency fund. They set their sights on clear milestones: $100 in the first month, $500 in three months, and aiming for $1,000 within six months. Together, they created a vibrant progress chart, giving each milestone a color and placing it prominently on the kitchen wall.

Innovative Contributions

Each member of the Rivera family found unique ways to contribute to the emergency fund:

- **Maria** offered tutoring sessions in math and science to younger students, dedicating a portion of her earnings to the fund.

- **Juan** is passionate about gardening. He sold plants and produce to neighbors and learned the value of hard work and savings.

- **Sofia**, with her infectious enthusiasm, initiated a lemonade stand that quickly became popular in their community.

- **Carmen** reviewed monthly expenses, identified opportunities to save on utilities and groceries, and occasionally worked overtime.

Milestones and Celebrations

Reaching the first milestone, the family indulged in a DIY spa day at home, pampering themselves with homemade masks and relaxation activities—a simple yet joyful reward for their collective effort. Juan is still unsure about what they did. Still, he enjoyed it (however, he will never admit that).

Upon hitting the $500 mark, they organized a storytelling night, during which each shared ghost stories around their outdoor fire pit while making s'mores.

Achieving the $1,000 goal was a momentous occasion. Carmen and the children decided on a day trip to a nearby national park, celebrating with nature walks and a picnic. This milestone was about the money saved, the lessons learned, and the stronger bond formed through shared goals and efforts.

Forward Together

The journey of building an emergency fund brought the Rivera family closer, teaching them the importance of preparation, collaboration, and the value of each contribution, no matter the size. It was a powerful lesson in financial literacy for Maria, Juan, and Sofia, showing them that even in a single-parent household, unity and perseverance could build a secure financial foundation. Inspired by their success, Carmen planned to continue nurturing this saving habit, setting new goals to ensure their emergency fund could cover even more future uncertainties.

The Rivera family's story emphasizes that financial preparedness is achievable through collective effort, creativity, and determination. The family structure in our case studies reflects the diversity of family dynamics and the universal importance of building a financial safety net.

Wrap-up: The Path to Financial Resilience

As we conclude our exploration of preparing for the unexpected, it's clear that financial preparedness is a cornerstone of a secure and stress-free family life. By taking proactive steps to build an emergency fund, choose the right insurance policies, and develop a comprehensive emergency plan, families can navigate life's uncertainties with confidence.

In our next chapter, we will focus on making financial discussions in your family a part of every day. Let's get going.

Proactive financial planning is about avoiding negative outcomes and creating a buffer that allows your family to face challenges without derailing your long-term financial goals.

Chapter 8

Conversations About Money

"Family conversations: where sarcasm is our love language, and laughter is our legacy." -Unknown

In the family life fabric, communication is the thread that binds relationships, fosters understanding and nurtures growth. Regarding finances, the importance of open, honest conversations cannot be overstated. Discussing money matters within the family setting is pivotal—not just for managing the household budget effectively but for laying the groundwork for a healthy financial future for all members.

Demystifying Finances

For many families, money remains a taboo topic, shrouded in secrecy or anxiety. However, breaking this silence is crucial. Open discussions about finances can demystify financial concepts, making them accessible and understandable to all family members, regardless of age. Such conversations help children and teenagers grasp the value of money, understand the importance of saving and investing, and recognize the realities of financial constraints and opportunities.

Beyond education, honest conversations about money can significantly enhance a family's approach to financial decision-making. When all members are informed and involved, decisions regarding savings, investments, and expenditures become more collective, deliberate, and aligned with the family's overall goals and values. This collaborative approach optimizes financial outcomes and reinforces trust and unity within the family.

Building a Foundation for the Future

Starting these conversations early sets the stage for lifelong financial literacy and responsibility. Children who grow up in environments where financial matters are openly discussed are better equipped to manage their finances independently, make informed decisions, and confidently navigate the complexities of the financial world.

As we delve deeper into this chapter, we will explore strategies for initiating and sustaining productive financial conversations within your family. From setting a positive tone and finding the right moments to talk about money to engaging children in budgeting exercises and planning for the future, we aim to provide practical advice and tools to help your family strengthen financial communication and decision-making.

Breaking the Ice: Starting Financial Conversations

Initiating conversations about money within the family can be manageable. Often, the best approach is to weave these discussions into the fabric of daily life, finding natural and relatable opportunities to broach the subject. Here are some strategies to help you break the ice and start meaningful financial conversations.

Finding the Right Moment

Timing can significantly impact the effectiveness of your financial discussions. Look for moments that naturally lend themselves to talking about money, such as:

- **During Budget Planning:** Involve the family in monthly budget planning sessions. It's a practical way to discuss income, expenses, and the importance of saving and planning for future goals.

- **After Receiving a Bill:** Use the arrival of a bill as a prompt to explain why you pay for certain services (like electricity or internet) and how these costs fit into the family budget. It's an opportunity to discuss the value of resources and the importance of mindful consumption.

Using Everyday Situations

Everyday life is filled with teachable moments that can help demystify financial concepts for children and encourage healthy discussions about money.

- **Grocery Shopping:** Turn a routine trip to the supermarket into a lesson on budgeting and making informed spending choices. Explain why you choose certain products over others, compare prices, and discuss the concept of value for money.

- **Planning a Family Outing:** Involve your children in planning a budget-friendly family outing. Discuss the costs associated with different activities and make decisions together on what you can afford. This teaches budgeting and prioritizes family time and making memories over spending money.

Creating a Safe Space for Questions

Encourage questions and curiosity about finances from all family members. Make it clear that no question is too simple or silly. Creating a safe and open discussion environment ensures children feel comfortable seeking information and advice about money matters.

Children learn a lot by observation. Demonstrate your teaching behaviors by making thoughtful financial decisions and discussing your thought process openly with your family. Your actions can serve as powerful lessons in financial responsibility.

Figure 8.1

Family Financial Discussion Tip Sheet

Introduction

Hello, Family! This sheet contains fun questions to help us talk about money together. It's like a treasure map that leads us to make smart money choices. Ready to explore? Let's go!

Section 1: Dream Big and Save

- What is something really cool you'd like to save money for?
- If you had $100, what would you do with it to help our family?
- What is a fun challenge we can do as a family to save money?
- What are small things we could spend less on, so we can save more for our big dreams?

Section 2: Wise Spending

- How do we decide if buying something big, like a video game or a bike, is worth it?
- Have you ever bought something and then wished you hadn't? What was it?
- What does it mean to be 'smart' about spending our money?
- Before we buy something big, what are three questions we should ask ourselves?

Section 3: Growing Our Piggy Banks

- What's something you'd like to save up for, just for yourself? Why is that important to you?
- How does putting a little money away all the time help us later?
- What creative way could we add more money to our savings jar this month?
- Why do you think having a 'just in case' money jar is a good idea?

Ready to discuss finances with the family? Where do you get started? We created a Family Financial Discussion Tip Sheet (Figure 8.1). You can download a copy of the form from the resource page at www.YourFamilyYourFinances.com/playbook-resources.

Starting financial conversations within the family sets the foundation for a lifetime of financial literacy and responsibility. By finding the right moments to discuss money matters and using everyday situations as teachable moments, you can help demystify finances for your children and strengthen your family's approach to financial decision-making.

Guidelines for Healthy Financial Discussions

Engaging in productive and positive financial discussions within the family is crucial for fostering an environment of trust, learning, and mutual respect. Here are some guidelines to ensure that conversations about money are healthy, informative, and inclusive.

Creating a Safe Space

The foundation of any meaningful financial discussion is a safe and supportive environment where all family members feel comfortable sharing their thoughts, questions, and concerns. Encourage an atmosphere where every family member, regardless of age, feels their input is valued. Emphasize listening as much as speaking, ensuring everyone's perspective is heard and respected. As with other discussions in this book, you must be open and nonjudgmental.

Instead of making every conversation about finances a special meeting, try integrating financial discussions into regular family meetings or conversations, making them a natural and expected part of family life. This normalcy helps to reduce any anxiety or discomfort around the topic.

Age-Appropriate Topics

Tailoring conversations to be age-appropriate ensures that children remain engaged and can comprehend the information being shared.

- **For Younger Children:** Focus on basic concepts like saving, earning, and the value of money through simple, relatable examples. Interactive activities or games can be particularly effective in conveying these ideas. Games like *Monopoly* and the *Game of Life* are great tools and fun for the whole family.

- **For Teenagers:** Discuss more complex topics such as budgeting, credit, and investing, connecting these concepts to their near-future realities like earning their first paycheck, saving for college, or buying their first car. The *Cashflow 101* game from Robert Kiyosaki's Rich Dad Poor Dad Company (https://amzn.to/3vBJVcz) can be a wonderful way to teach teenagers (and you) about cash flow and passive income.

Avoiding Financial Taboos

Breaking down the barriers around discussing money is essential for building financial literacy and confidence in managing finances. When possible, share appropriate details about household finances, including how budgets are planned and the importance of saving and investing for the future. This openness can demystify children's financial management. Sharing past financial challenges and how they were overcome can be incredibly educational. It teaches resilience, problem-solving, and the importance of planning.

Encouraging Questions and Curiosity

Create an environment where asking questions about money is encouraged. This curiosity can lead to a deeper understanding and interest in financial matters.

- **There are No Stupid Questions:** Reinforce that every question is valid. A question asked is an opportunity to learn and grow.

- **Share Learning Resources:** Recommend books, websites, and other resources that family members can explore independently to learn more about finances.

Figure 8.2

Guide to Fostering Healthy Financial Discussions Within the Family

Introduction:
Engaging in open and positive financial conversations within the family is crucial for teaching financial literacy, instilling responsibility, and preparing for future financial independence. This expanded guide provides detailed strategies and examples to help families discuss money matters in an engaging, educational, and age-appropriate manner.

1. Creating a Safe Space for Financial Conversations

- **Start with Positivity:** Kick off financial discussions by talking about exciting financial goals the family has achieved or is working towards, such as a vacation or a new family car. This emphasizes the benefits of financial planning and saving.
- **Encourage Questions:** Create a "question jar" where family members can drop in their financial questions anonymously, and dedicate time during family meetings to answer them. This can help shy members feel more comfortable participating.
- **Share Experiences:** Parents might share a story about their first savings account, including how they felt when they saved enough for something important to them, demonstrating the emotional reward of saving.
- **Reassure Confidentiality:** Establish a family rule that what is discussed in family financial meetings stays within the family, reinforcing trust and security.

2. Making Financial Topics Age-Appropriate

- **Simplify Concepts:** Use a lemonade stand example to explain profit and expenses to younger children. For teens, compare a budget to planning a party, where they must balance the cost of food, decorations, and activities without overspending.
- **Visual Aids:** For younger children, use board games like Monopoly to introduce them to concepts of money management, investment, and even the randomness of financial success and setbacks. For older children, you might want to use something like Robert Kiyosaki's Cashflow Game (https://amzn.to/3IxiKTk). It is

If there is one thing that you can get from this chapter, it is that we need to have healthy financial discussions with our families. We have created a guide to help you have some ideas in mind while you are communicating with your family (Figure 8.2). You can get this copy from the book's resource page: www.YourFamilyYourFinances.com/playbook-resources.

By adhering to these guidelines, families can cultivate a culture of open and healthy financial discussions. Such conversations enhance financial literacy and preparedness and strengthen family bonds through shared goals and mutual support. Encouraging transparency, respect, and continuous learning about money matters lays the groundwork for a financially savvy and resilient family unit.

Involving Children in Financial Planning

Incorporating children into the family's financial planning process is not just about teaching them the mechanics of money management; it's about instilling values, such as the importance of saving, the benefits of delayed gratification, and the empowerment that comes from making informed decisions. Here's how to effectively involve children in setting financial goals and understanding the rationale behind financial decisions.

Setting Financial Goals Together

Making children a part of setting financial goals helps them grasp the concept of working towards something meaningful, be it a family vacation, a new game console, or contributions to their college fund. Hold regular family meetings dedicated to discussing financial goals. Ensure everyone, including the children, has a voice in the conversation. This can be as simple as deciding on a savings goal for a family treat or as significant as planning for next year's vacation.

Create a visual representation of your goals, such as a chart or a jar that fills up as you save. This tangible representation can help children understand progress and see the direct results of saving.

Explaining Financial Decisions

Children are naturally curious, and explaining the thought process behind financial decisions can give them valuable insights into responsible money management. When discussing financial decisions, simplify the concepts to match the child's age and understanding. For instance, explain that saving for a vacation means the family has a unique experience to look forward to, which is more valuable than buying small toys now. Use everyday decisions to explain the concept of opportunity cost. For example, choosing between dining out and saving that money for a future goal. Highlight that every choice has benefits and costs, helping them understand the value of prioritizing their spending.

Apply these discussions to real-life scenarios to reinforce the lessons. For instance, involve your children in budgeting for a grocery trip, explaining why you choose certain items over others based on price and necessity. Or, if saving for something big, show them the budget and how their sacrifices contribute to the family reaching its goal.

Recognize and praise their contributions and understanding. Small rewards or acknowledgments for being part of the financial planning process can motivate continued interest and involvement.

Figure 8.3

It is important for your kids to feel like they have some control over their finances. We created a sheet for the younger kids to track their goals (Figure 8.3). It allows them to be creative and own their part of the family finances. You can download the sheet from the resource section of the website www.YourFamilyYourFinances.com/Playbook-resources.

By involving children in financial planning and decision-making, families teach valuable life skills and foster a sense of unity and shared purpose. By setting goals together and explaining the reasoning behind financial choices, children learn to appreciate the value of money, the importance of saving, and the satisfaction of achieving goals as a family.

Activity: Weekly Financial Check-Ins

Establishing a weekly family financial meeting can transform how your family approaches money management. These check-ins serve as a platform for open discussion, goal tracking, and financial education, ensuring everyone, from the adults to the youngest members, plays a role in the family's financial well-being. Here's how to make these meetings both productive and engaging.

Structure and Content

- **Set a Regular Time:** Choose a consistent time each week that works for everyone, such as Sunday evenings, to sit down together without distractions.

- **Agenda:** Have a loose agenda to keep the meeting focused. Topics might include.

  - Reviewing weekly spending.

  - Discussing savings goals.

  - Planning for upcoming expenses.

  - Any financial concerns or questions?

- **Keep It Short and Sweet:** Aim for the meetings to last up to 30 minutes to keep everyone's attention and ensure discussions remain engaging and to the point.

Role of Children

Involving children in these meetings educates them about financial management. It gives them a sense of ownership and responsibility towards family finances.

- **Savings Report:** Encourage children to report on their personal savings progress, share what they're saving for, and discuss any challenges they face.

- **Budget-Friendly Ideas:** Assign children the task of coming up with budget-friendly activity ideas for the family. This encourages creativity and teaches them to consider cost when planning fun activities.

These weekly check-ins are a valuable opportunity to reflect on the family's financial habits, celebrate successes, and identify areas for improvement.

- **Review Spending:** Briefly review the past week's spending, highlighting areas where the family did well and where you can cut back.

- **Celebrate Successes:** Acknowledge and celebrate when savings goals are met or when good financial decisions lead to positive outcomes. This could be as simple as sticking to the grocery budget or saving on utility bills.

- **Set Mini-Goals for Improvement:** If areas for improvement are identified, set mini-goals for the coming week, such as reducing discretionary spending or researching more affordable options for planned purchases.

Weekly Check-In Template

Figure 8.4

Weekly Financial Check-In Template

Family Name:
Date of Check-In:

1. Agenda Topics:

- Brief Overview of This Week's Financial Highlights
- Upcoming Financial Events or Needs

2. Savings Updates:

- Current Total Savings Balance:
  (Include any interest earned if applicable)
- Contributions This Week:
  - Amount:
  - Source(s):
- Progress Towards Specific Goals:
  (e.g., emergency fund, vacation, education)
  - Goal:
  - Amount Saved This Week:
  - Total Saved Towards Goal:
  - Remaining to Goal Target:

3. Spending Review:

- Total Spending This Week:
- Breakdown by Category:
  - Essentials (Groceries, Bills, etc.):
  - Discretionary (Entertainment, Eating Out):
  - Unexpected Expenses:
- Reflection:
  - Did we stay within our planned budget?

Copyright 2024 - CPTX Media LLC

Here is a Template (Figure 8.4) to help guide you and your family through your weekly financial check-ins. As always, you can download it from our resource site at www.Your FamilyYourFinances.com/playbook-resources.

By making financial check-ins a regular part of family life, you're managing money better and fostering open communication, financial literacy, and teamwork. These meetings become a space where financial goals are shared and pursued collectively, where each family member, regardless of age, contributes to the family's financial health and learns valuable lessons along the way.

Case Study: The Lee Family and Financial Goal-Setting

Meet the Lee family: Angela, David, and their children, Kevin (9) and Emma (13). Growing up in the San Francisco Bay area, Angela and David grew up in traditional families with little influence on family money decisions. They decided that they wanted this to be different for their children. The Lees believe in the importance of financial literacy and want to ensure their children understand how to manage money wisely. To this end, they decided to actively involve Kevin and Emma in the family's financial planning process.

Initiating Financial Conversations

Angela and David introduced the concept of financial goal-setting during a casual family dinner. They discussed the family's dreams and aspirations, such as taking a summer vacation to a national park and purchasing a new family computer. By framing these aspirations as shared goals, the conversation naturally led to discussions about saving and budgeting.

Setting Goals Together

The family decided to make their financial planning more interactive by creating a "Goals Board" in the living room. Kevin and Emma were encouraged to add their own goals, with Kevin wishing for a new bicycle and Emma saving for a digital drawing tablet. Each goal was accompanied by a savings tracker, which the family would update together.

Explaining Financial Decisions

Whenever Angela and David had to make significant financial decisions, they took the opportunity to explain their thought process to the children. For instance, they discussed the concept of opportunity cost and the value of experiences over immediate gratification when choosing to save extra money for the vacation fund instead of dining out.

Involvement in Budgeting

The Lees involved Kevin and Emma in budgeting for the family's grocery shopping to make the process hands-on. They explained why they chose certain brands over others and how buying in bulk or choosing seasonal produce could save money. This exercise helped the children understand practical budgeting and the impact of small savings over time.

Realizing Their Goals

After months of collective saving and learning, the family decided to take a vacation to the national park. Kevin also earned his bicycle by contributing to household chores and saving his allowance. In contrast, Emma saved enough for her drawing tablet by doing extra tutoring for younger students.

Reflection and Growth

The experience brought the Lee family closer and taught Kevin and Emma invaluable lessons about financial responsibility, teamwork, and the satisfaction of achieving goals through perseverance. Angela and David noted significant growth in their children's understanding of money management and enthusiasm for participating in financial decisions.

The Lee family's journey illustrates the power of involving children in financial planning and decision-making. By engaging in open conversations, setting goals together, and providing real-life applications, Angela and David equipped Kevin and Emma with the tools and knowledge to navigate their financial futures confidently. This case study is an inspiring example for other families looking to foster financial literacy and shared responsibility from an early age.

Wrap-Up: Fostering a Culture of Financial Openness

The Power of Financial Dialogue

By breaking the ice on financial topics, setting financial goals together, and holding regular financial check-ins, families can transform their approach to money management. These practices encourage a culture of financial openness, where:

- **Learning is Continuous:** Financial literacy is built daily, conversation by conversation. Every discussion is an opportunity to learn something new or see things differently.

- **Responsibility is Shared:** When children are involved in financial planning and decision-making, they learn to take responsibility for their financial habits early on, setting them up for a lifetime of sound money management.

- **Resilience is Built:** Open conversations about money prepare families to face financial challenges together, strengthening their resilience and ability to navigate uncertainties.

To continue growing in your financial journey, remember that resources are available to support you beyond these conversations:

- **Visit YourFamilyYourFinances.com** for a wealth of articles, tools, and resources designed to deepen your understanding and enhance your family's financial practices.

- **Tune into relevant episodes of *Your Family Your Finances*** to hear expert advice, real-life stories, and practical tips that complement the strategies discussed in this chapter.

Final Thoughts

In closing, remember that conversations about money are about more than just numbers on a page; they're about aligning your family's financial practices with your values, goals, and dreams. They're about empowering each family member, regardless of age, with the knowledge and confidence to make informed financial decisions. Most importantly, they're about strengthening the bonds between family members through shared goals and mutual support.

As you continue to navigate your family's financial journey, let openness, honesty, and collaboration be your guiding principles. Here's to a future where financial conversations are not just common but are a cherished and integral part of family life, leading to informed decisions, fulfilling goals, and a legacy of financial savvy passed down through generations.

For many families, money remains a taboo topic, shrouded in secrecy or anxiety. However, breaking this silence is crucial. Open discussions about finances can demystify financial concepts, making them accessible and understandable to all family members, regardless of age.

Chapter 9

Using Financial Tools And Resources

"Give me a lever long enough and a fulcrum on which to place it, and I shall move the world." -Archimedes.

In today's digital age, managing family finances has never been more accessible or efficient, thanks to a wealth of financial tools and resources at our fingertips. These tools are designed to simplify the number-crunching aspects of financial management and empower families with the knowledge and insights needed to make informed decisions and achieve their financial goals.

The Digital Advantage

The array of financial tools available today can automate many tedious tasks that traditionally made financial management seem daunting. From budgeting apps that track spending in real-time, to investment platforms that demystify the stock market, these resources transform how families approach their finances.

Benefits include:

- **Simplification:** Automated tools take the hassle out of tasks like budgeting, bill payments, and tracking investments, allowing families to focus more on strategy and less on paperwork.

- **Insights:** Many financial apps and websites offer analytics and personalized insights, helping families understand their spending habits, identify potential savings, and adjust their financial plans.

- **Education:** Beyond managing money, these tools often provide educational resources that enhance financial literacy, covering everything from basic budgeting principles to complex investment strategies.

Fostering Financial Literacy

One of the most significant benefits of modern financial tools is their role in fostering financial literacy among all family members. By making financial concepts accessible and engaging, these tools can demystify the world of finance, making it easier for even young family members to grasp important principles and participate in financial decision-making. The landscape of financial tools and resources is vast and varied, catering to different needs, goals, and levels of expertise. Whether you're looking for a simple budgeting app, a comprehensive financial planning platform, or educational resources to grow your financial knowledge, there's likely a tool out there that fits the bill.

As we delve deeper into this chapter, we'll explore some of the most popular and practical financial tools and resources available to families today. We'll guide you in choosing the right tools for your family's needs, using them effectively, and integrating them into your daily financial management practices. With the right tools, your family can streamline its financial operations, gain valuable insights into your financial health, and take meaningful steps toward achieving your financial dreams.

Overview of Financial Tools

Various financial tools have been developed in the digital era to address virtually every aspect of personal and family finance. Here's a closer look at some categories of these tools and how they can benefit your family.

Budgeting Apps and Software

Popular Choices: Apps like Mint, YNAB (You Need A Budget), and PocketGuard have become household names for managing finances. Each offers unique features to cater to different budgeting styles and goals.

Benefits: These tools excel in making budgeting accessible and manageable. They can automatically categorize transactions, set budgets for different spending categories, send alerts when you're approaching your spending limit, and generate financial reports to give you an overview of your finances.

Investment Platforms

User-Friendly Platforms: With the rise of robo-advisors like Betterment and Wealthfront, alongside platforms like Robinhood and Acorns, investing has never been more accessible. These platforms often come with minimal fees and user-friendly interfaces, which are ideal for beginners.

Educational Resources: Many investment platforms offer educational materials tailored for beginners, making them an excellent resource for families looking to learn about investing together.

Savings Tools

Online Savings Accounts: Many online banks offer high-yield savings accounts with interest rates significantly higher than traditional banks, helping your savings grow faster.

Apps That Round Up Purchases: Apps like Acorns round up your everyday purchases to the nearest dollar and invest the difference, making saving almost effortless.

Financial Planning Software

Comprehensive Planning: Software like Quicken or Personal Capital provides tools for budgeting, investment tracking, and long-term financial planning, including retirement and education savings, for those looking for a more holistic approach to their finances.

Benefits: These platforms offer a comprehensive view of your financial life, making it easier to set long-term goals and track progress.

Figure 9.1

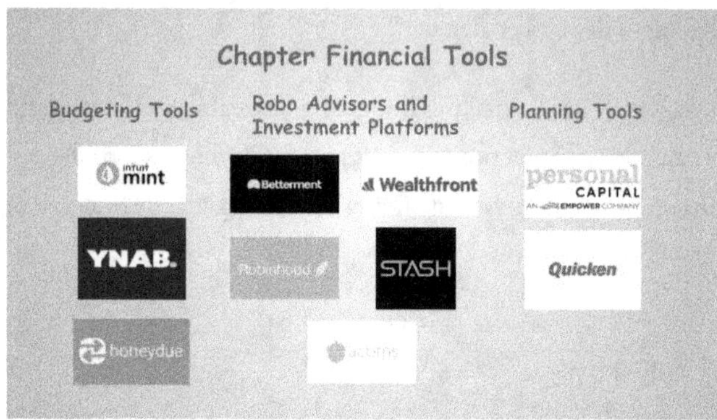

With the advent of the Internet and Financial Technology (FinTech), hundreds of options are available to help you track your finances. Figure 9.1 above gives a few examples of our favorite platforms. Always check our website at www.YourFamilyYourFinances.com to get our most up-to-date resources.

Navigating the world of personal finance can be daunting, but managing your family's finances can become easier and more effective with the right tools. By utilizing budgeting apps, investment platforms, savings tools, and financial planning software, families can gain greater control over their finances, make informed decisions, and work collaboratively toward achieving their financial goals. Each tool offers unique benefits, whether it simplifies daily budgeting tasks, introduces you to the world of investing, boosts your savings efforts, or helps you plan for the future. The key is to explore and find the ones that align with your family's needs and financial aspirations.

Choosing the Right Tools for Your Family

With the vast array of financial tools available, selecting the ones that best fit your family's needs can seem overwhelming. Here's a guide to making informed choices that align with your financial situation and goals.

Assessing Needs and Goals

Before exploring the myriad financial tools available, take a step back and assess your family's unique needs and goals.

- **Identify Your Objectives:** Are you looking to track daily spending, save for a family vacation, invest for the future, or perhaps all of the above? Different tools serve different purposes, so knowing your goals can help narrow your options.

- **Consider Your Financial Situation:** A perfect tool for one family might not be suitable for another. For example, families building their savings might benefit more from a simple budgeting app than comprehensive investment software.

Privacy and Security

Privacy and security are paramount in the digital age, especially concerning sensitive financial information. Look for financial tools with robust security features like encryption, two-factor authentication, and regular security audits. Check user feedback, which can provide insights into the tool's reliability and security. Also, check for any history of data breaches or security issues.

Ease of Use

A tool's effectiveness is greatly improved if it's simple enough for regular use.

User Interface: Look for a tool with an intuitive, user-friendly interface. Many apps offer free trials or demos, a great way to test usability.

Integration with Daily Life: Consider how well the tool fits into your family's routine. For instance, a budgeting app that can sync with your bank accounts and credit cards can save time and ensure accuracy in tracking expenses.

Figure 9.2

Family Financial Tools Checklist

Introduction
Choosing the right financial tools for your family is crucial in managing your finances effectively. This checklist outlines the key factors to consider, ensuring you select tools that align with your family's needs, prioritize security, and are user-friendly. Use this visual aid as a guide when evaluating your options.

1. Assessing Needs and Goals

- ☐ **Identify Financial Goals:** Determine what you want to achieve with your financial tools (e.g., budget tracking, savings goals, investment monitoring).
- ☐ **Budget Management:** Look for tools that offer comprehensive budgeting features, including the ability to categorize expenses and set spending limits.
- ☐ **Savings Tracking:** Ensure the tool can track multiple savings goals, showing progress over time.
- ☐ **Investment Assistance:** If applicable, select tools that offer investment tracking and insights.

2. Evaluating Privacy and Security Features

- ☐ **Data Encryption:** Confirm that the tool uses strong encryption to protect your financial data.
- ☐ **Two-Factor Authentication (2FA):** Check for the availability of 2FA to add an extra layer of security to your accounts.
- ☐ **Privacy Policy:** Review the tool's privacy policy to understand how your data will be used and protected.
- ☐ **Regular Updates:** Ensure the tool receives regular updates to maintain security measures and add new features.

3. Ensuring Ease of Use

- ☐ **User-Friendly Interface:** Select a tool with an intuitive interface that all family members can navigate easily.

Choosing the right financial tools for your family is extremely important. To help you and your family evaluate the different options, we have created a checklist for you to use (Figure 9.2). You can download the form from our website at www.YourFamilyYourFin ances.com/Playbook-resources. You can also find our most current recommendations for tools there.

Selecting the right financial tools for your family doesn't have to be a daunting task. By carefully assessing your needs and goals, paying close attention to privacy and security features, and prioritizing ease of use, you can identify the tools that best support your family's financial journey. Remember, the goal is not to use every tool available but to find those that genuinely make managing your finances easier, more effective, and more aligned with your family's aspirations.

Educational Resources for Financial Learning

While financial tools can significantly aid in managing your family's finances, coupling these tools with a solid foundation of financial knowledge is key to making the most informed decisions. Some educational resources can help enhance your family's financial literacy.

Books and eBooks

A well-curated selection of books can provide invaluable insights into all facets of personal finance. Consider adding these to your reading list:

- **For Beginners:** *The Total Money Makeover* by Dave Ramsey offers a straightforward approach to budgeting, debt reduction, and financial planning.

- **For Kids:** *The Everything Kids' Money Book* by Brette Sember introduces children to the basics of money management in an engaging and accessible way.

- **For Adults:** John C. Bogle's *The Little Book of Common Sense Investing* provides a primer on the importance of low-cost index fund investing.

Online Courses and Webinars

Many platforms offer online courses and webinars that cater to different learning styles and schedules, making them a flexible option for families.

- **Coursera & Udemy (www.coursera.com) (www.udemy.com):** These platforms feature courses on various financial topics taught by industry experts, from personal finance basics to more advanced investment strategies.

- **Khan Academy (www.khanacademy.com):** Offers free courses on personal finance and economics, perfect for beginners and young learners.

Financial Blogs and Podcasts

Staying updated with financial blogs and podcasts is a great way to continually learn about managing finances, discovering new strategies, and keeping abreast of financial trends.

- **Blogs:** Websites like NerdWallet (www.nerdwallet.com) offer a wealth of articles on everything from frugal living to retirement planning.

- **Podcasts:** "So Money with Farnoosh Torabi" and "The Dave Ramsey Show" provide insightful discussions on personal finance topics, success stories, and practical tips.

Leveraging Local Resources

Pay attention to the resources available in your own community. Libraries often have a section dedicated to personal finance books and magazines, and community centers might host free financial planning workshops. Empowering your family with financial knowledge is as crucial as managing your finances with the right tools.

You and your family can build a robust understanding of personal finance by exploring books, engaging with online courses and webinars, and regularly following reputable financial blogs and podcasts. This continual learning process enriches your financial literacy. It enhances your capacity to make sound financial decisions, ensuring your family's secure and prosperous future.

Activity: Financial Resource Exploration Day

Creating a financially savvy family requires individual knowledge and discipline, collective exploration, and decision-making. A Financial Resource Exploration Day is a perfect way to engage every family member in discovering the vast world of financial tools and resources, making it a collaborative and educational experience. Here's how to organize this productive and fun day.

Research Phase

Start with a family meeting to outline the day's objective and assign tasks based on each member's interests and the family's financial goals.

- **Set Clear Objectives:** Discuss what you hope to achieve, whether finding a better budget, learning about investing, or discovering resources for financial education.

- **Assign Research Areas:** Each family member chooses a financial tool or resource to research. Assignments can be based on personal interest or the family's current financial needs, ensuring a wide range of topics are covered.

Presentation

After the research phase, reconvene for a family meeting where each member presents their findings. This can be an informal and fun way to share your learning.

- **Pros and Cons:** Encourage each presenter to discuss the tool or resource they researched's benefits and potential drawbacks.

- **Practical Application:** Discuss how the tool or resource could be practically applied to benefit the family's finances.

Decision-Making

With all the information presented, it's time to decide which tools or resources to adopt as a family. Consider each option's pros and cons and how well it aligns with your family's goals. A democratic vote can be an effective way to make the final decision. For the selected tools, proceed to setting up accounts or downloading apps. Involve the whole family to foster a sense of ownership and commitment. Use this opportunity to explore new tools and reflect on your current financial habits and how these new resources might improve or augment them.

Figure 9.3

Financial Resource Exploration Day Planner & Checklist

Introduction

A Financial Resource Exploration Day is a dedicated time for your family to discover and evaluate various financial tools, resources, and strategies to enhance financial literacy and management. This planner and checklist will guide you through organizing an effective exploration day, from research to decision-making.

Preparation Phase

- ☐ **Set a Date:** Choose a day that works for all family members to ensure full participation.
- ☐ **Assign Roles:** Designate specific tasks to each family member (research, presentation, note-taking).
- ☐ **Define Objectives:** Clearly outline what you hope to achieve by the end of the day (e.g., selecting a new budgeting app and understanding investment options).

Research Phase

- ☐ **Select Topics:** Identify key financial areas you want to explore (budgeting, saving, investing, etc.).
- ☐ **Gather Resources:** Collect information from reputable sources (books, websites, financial blogs, and podcasts).
- ☐ **Prepare Questions:** List questions or concerns you want the exploration to address for each topic.

Presentation Phase

- ☐ **Divide Topics:** Assign a topic to each family member for research and presentation.
- ☐ **Choose Presentation Tools:** Decide on how each member will present their findings (slide presentation, handouts, verbal summary).
- ☐ **Practice Presentations:** Allow time for each presenter to practice and refine their presentation.

To help you with your Financial Resource Exploration Activity, we have compiled a planner and checklist for you and your family (Figure 9.3). You can download the planner from the book resource site at www.YourFamilyYourFinances.com/playbook-resources.

Engaging in a Financial Resource Exploration Day helps families discover tools and resources that can enhance their financial management and strengthen family bonds through shared learning and decision-making. By making financial education a collaborative and ongoing effort, families can build a stronger, more informed foundation for their financial future.

Case Study: The Grant Family's Financial Resource Exploration Day

Meet the Grant family: Diana and Marcus, along with their four children: Ava (15), Noah (13), Liam (10), and Zoe (7). Understanding the importance of financial literacy and keen on improving their family's financial management, they dedicated a day to exploring and evaluating financial tools and resources. They called it the "Financial Resource Exploration Day."

Initiating the Exploration

The Grants wanted each family member to participate actively in their financial journey. They decided everyone would research a financial tool or resource to help achieve the family's diverse financial goals, from budgeting and savings to investing and learning about finances.

- **Ava**, interested in how to fund college, searched for apps and websites focused on education savings accounts and scholarship opportunities.

- **Noah**, a budding tech enthusiast, was looking for budgeting apps that could help the family allocate funds to save for a family vacation.

- **Liam**, curious about how money grows, decided to investigate beginner-friendly investment platforms that offer resources for young savers.

- **Zoe**, with a bit of help from her parents, aimed to find a fun, interactive app that introduces kids to basic concepts of money, saving, and spending through games.

Family Presentations

On their designated day, the Grants gathered with excitement. Each member presented their findings, discussing each tool or resource's potential benefits and limitations and how it could integrate into or enhance the family's financial strategy.

- **Ava** introduced a comprehensive platform for managing education savings, highlighting its features for tracking savings goals and finding scholarships.

- **Noah** showcased a budgeting app that tracks expenses and motivates the family toward their saving goals with visual progress charts and spending alerts.

- **Liam** found an investment app that simplifies the world of stocks and bonds for beginners and provides educational content tailored for young investors.

- **Zoe** delighted everyone with a colorful, engaging app that teaches kids about earning, saving, and spending, making learning about money fun and interactive.

Reflecting on the Day

The Grant family's Financial Resource Exploration Day was a meaningful venture that went beyond just finding the right tools. It was an exercise in collaboration, education, and shared responsibility towards the family's financial health. Each member felt more empowered and invested in their collective financial future. This experience enhanced their understanding of personal finance. It strengthened their family bond and commitment to supporting each other's goals and dreams.

Wrap-Up: Empowering Your Family's Financial Journey

As we conclude this chapter on harnessing financial tools and resources, it's clear that the right mix of technology and knowledge can significantly empower your family's financial journey. From budgeting apps that simplify daily expense tracking to investment platforms that demystify the stock market, these tools are invaluable allies in achieving economic stability and growth.

The digital age has brought financial management into the palms of our hands, offering unprecedented access to tools that can automate, educate, and inspire. By carefully selecting and utilizing these resources, your family can:

- **Streamline Financial Tasks:** Automate the mundane aspects of financial management, freeing up time to focus on strategic decisions and family discussions about financial priorities and goals.

- **Enhance Financial Literacy:** Use educational platforms to deepen your understanding of financial concepts, ensuring that every family member, from adults to children, is equipped with the knowledge to make informed decisions.

- **Foster a Proactive Financial Mindset:** Leverage tools that provide insights into spending habits, investment performance, and savings progress to cultivate a mindset geared towards proactive financial planning and goal achievement.

Choosing Wisely and Learning Continuously

Selecting the right tools for your family is a critical step. Still, it's equally important to remain engaged and open to learning. As your family's financial needs evolve, so too might the tools that best suit your circumstances. Regularly revisiting your choices and staying informed about new resources can ensure that your family's approach to financial management remains effective and aligned with your goals.

The Journey Ahead

Remember, the journey to financial well-being is ongoing. While tools and resources can provide support and guidance, the core of this journey is your family's commitment to open communication, shared learning, and mutual support. Encourage curiosity, celebrate milestones, and embrace challenges as opportunities for growth. With the right tools in hand and a solid foundation of financial literacy, your family can navigate the complexities of personal finance with confidence and grace.

As you move forward, keep exploring, learning, and discussing. The financial tools and resources world constantly expands, offering new opportunities to enhance your family's economic health and well-being. Here's to a future where your family not only achieves its financial goals but thrives, empowered by knowledge, technology, and a shared vision of success.

As we move into the book's final chapter, we will begin to wrap up our journey together. This will also be the beginning of a long financial journey with your family. My goal is that this will not just be a journey for your immediate family but also for all of your following generations.

One of the most significant benefits of modern financial tools is their role in fostering financial literacy among all family members. By making financial concepts accessible and engaging, these tools can demystify the world of finance, making it easier for even young family members to grasp important principles and participate in financial decision-making.

Chapter 10

Your Family's Financial Journey

"The journey of a thousand miles begins with a single step." - Lao Tzu

As we reach the culmination of our journey through the *Family Finance Playbook,* we must pause and reflect on the significant strides we've made together. This journey has been about more than just understanding the mechanics of money; it has been a comprehensive exploration to enhance your family's financial literacy and practices.

Reflection on Learning

Throughout this book, we've delved into various essential aspects of personal finance, each designed to equip your family with the knowledge and skills needed for a prosperous financial future:

1. **Introduction:** We emphasize the importance of financial literacy in family life and the transformative power of informed financial decisions.

2. **Budgeting and Planning:** Understanding how to manage your income and expenses effectively lays the foundation for financial stability and goal achievement.

3. **Earning and Saving:** We explored strategies for maximizing income and the critical role savings play in securing your family's future.

4. **Investing:** The chapters on investing demystify the process and show how informed investment choices can grow a family's wealth over time.

5. **Preparing for the Unexpected:** We underscored the importance of readiness for life's uncertainties, highlighting the need for an emergency fund and insurance.

6. **Financial Tools and Resources:** Exploring modern tools and educational resources showcased how technology can simplify financial management and enhance learning.

The Value of Financial Literacy

This journey reaffirmed that financial literacy is invaluable. It extends beyond financial health to empower families to make decisions that resonate deeply with their values and aspirations. Financial literacy fosters a sense of security, enables goal fulfillment, and prepares families to navigate financial challenges confidently.

Financial education is a lifelong endeavor, with each step taken enhancing the family's ability to engage in thoughtful financial planning, informed decision-making, and pursuing financial goals that align with their deepest values. The principles and strategies outlined throughout this book aim to inform and inspire action and ongoing engagement with personal finance as a dynamic and integral part of family life.

Creating Your Family's Financial Action Plan

After journeying through financial literacy and management, the next vital step is to apply these insights through a concrete, actionable plan that's tailored to your family's unique situation and aspirations. Here's how you can craft a financial action plan that reflects your family's priorities, translates goals into actionable steps, and builds a supportive ecosystem for sustained progress. Your family's financial action plan begins with setting clear priorities. Reflect on the lessons and strategies you've encountered:

- **Assess Your Financial Landscape:** Take stock of your current financial situation, including income, debts, savings, and investments.

- **Identify Your Goals:** Define what you want to achieve, from short-term objectives like vacation savings, to long-term goals like retirement or college funds for your children.

- **Prioritize Based on Impact and Urgency:** Some goals will naturally take precedence due to their immediate impact or urgency. Prioritizing these will help focus your efforts and resources effectively.

Action Steps

With your priorities set, the next phase is delineating these goals into tangible, achievable steps.

1. **Break Down Each Goal:** Divide larger goals into smaller, manageable tasks. For example, start with a monthly savings target if you want to build an emergency fund.

2. **Assign Responsibilities:** Make financial planning a family affair. Assign tasks or areas of responsibility to family members based on their interests and capabilities.

3. **Set Deadlines:** Establish realistic timelines for each goal and task. Deadlines serve as motivation and help track progress.

Building a Support System

Achieving financial goals is a journey that benefits immensely from a supportive environment. Cultivating a network of encouragement and accountability can enhance your family's commitment and resilience.

- **Foster Family Engagement:** Regular family meetings to discuss progress, address challenges, and adjust plans as necessary, can keep everyone aligned and motivated.

- **Join Financial Communities:** Connect with broader communities that share your financial interests and goals, such as online forums, local clubs, or financial literacy workshops. These networks can offer valuable advice, motivation, and a sense of belonging.

- **Celebrate Milestones:** Acknowledge and celebrate achievements, no matter how small. Recognizing progress reinforces commitment and motivates continued effort toward your financial goals.

Figure 10.1

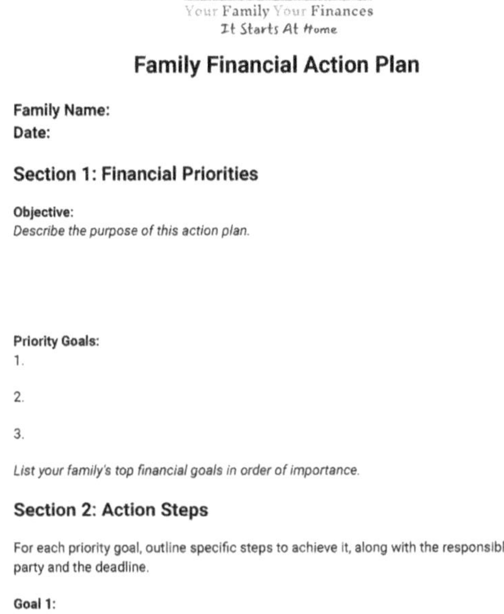

Okay, it's time for your final exam. We created a catch-all document for you to create your Family Financial Action Plan (Figure 10.1). You can always download a copy from our resource site at www.YourFamilyYourFinances.com/Playbook-resources.

Creating a financial action plan is a dynamic process that adapts as your family's needs and goals evolve. By setting clear priorities, breaking goals into actionable steps, and building a supportive network, your family can confidently navigate the path to financial success. Remember, the journey toward financial well-being is ongoing, and each step forward is a building block for your family's future prosperity.

To create your plan, you will use all the tools and sheets you have created throughout this book. The Family Financial Action Plan is the culmination of what you have learned throughout this book. If you would like to see me walk you through this entire process, I recorded a Master Class on the resources page for this book. Go to www.yourfamilyyou rfinances.com/playbook-resources to see the walkthrough.

Encouraging Continuous Engagement

As we underscored throughout our journey, pursuing financial literacy and wellness is not a destination but a continuous, evolving path. It's a commitment to lifelong learning and adaptation in response to the ever-changing financial landscapes and life stages. Here's how your family can remain engaged and proactive in this ongoing journey.

The financial world is dynamic, with new opportunities, tools, and challenges emerging constantly. Staying informed and adaptable is key to successfully navigating these changes. Regularly update your financial education by reading books, attending workshops, or enrolling in online courses. The landscape of personal finance continually evolves, and staying informed is crucial for making sound decisions. We will share various financial techniques and strategies through our blog site, www.yourfamilyyourfinances.com, and the *Your Family Your Finances* Show on YourHomeTV. All of that information can be found on our website. Be open to adjusting your financial strategies as your family's needs and goals evolve. What works today may be less effective tomorrow, so flexibility is essential.

Staying Connected

In the digital age, support and information are just a click away. Engaging with online communities and resources can provide both motivation and valuable insights.

- **Visit YourFamilyYourFinances.com:** Our platform is continually updated with the latest financial education, tools, and resources. It's designed to support you at every stage of your financial journey, offering practical advice, insights, and encouragement.

- **Engage with the Community:** Connecting with others on the same financial path, whether through social media, online forums, or local groups, can provide a wealth of support and inspiration. We encourage you to interact with others through our *Your Family Your Finances* Facebook Group (www.facebook.co m/yourfamilyyourfinances). Sharing experiences, successes, and challenges with the *Your Family Your Finances* community can reinforce your commitment and offer diverse financial management perspectives.

Building a Culture of Financial Well-being

Encouraging continuous engagement in financial education and community support fosters a culture of financial well-being within your family. It reinforces that managing finances is not just about numbers but about making choices that reflect your values, support your goals, and enhance your life.

Remember that your family's financial journey is unique and enriched by your specific goals, challenges, and triumphs. By committing to ongoing learning, staying adaptable, and leveraging the support of communities like *Your Family Your Finances,* you equip your family with the tools to navigate the financial aspects of life with confidence and grace. Here's to a future where financial literacy and wellness are integral to your family's legacy, continually evolving and enriching your lives together.

Final Words of Encouragement

As we draw this guide closer, you must recognize your embarked journey. The path to financial literacy and empowerment is both challenging and rewarding, and by engaging with *Your Family Your Finances,* you've taken a significant step toward securing a brighter financial future for your family.

Taking control of your financial future is an empowering act. It's about more than just numbers and budgets; it's about making choices that align with your family's values, aspirations, and goals. Celebrate your progress thus far, no matter how small it may seem. Each step forward is a building block towards greater financial resilience and independence. Remember, empowerment comes from action—every decision you make, every goal you set, and every challenge you overcome strengthens your family's financial foundation.

Your journey doesn't end here. As you continue to learn, grow, and navigate the complexities of personal finance, remember that you're part of a larger community of families on similar paths. Sharing your experiences, successes, and challenges with the *Your Family Your Finances* community can be incredibly rewarding. Not only does it offer you a chance to reflect on your journey, but it also provides encouragement and inspiration to others.

Looking Ahead

As you progress, remember the principles and strategies you've learned and stay open to new ideas, tools, and resources. The financial landscape is ever-evolving, and staying engaged and informed is key to navigating it successfully. Remember, financial literacy is not a destination but a journey—one that requires curiosity, adaptability, and persistence.

Thank you for allowing *Your Family Your Finances* to join your family's journey toward financial literacy and empowerment. Here's to your continued success, resilience, and growth. Let's continue to learn, share, and build a financially secure future together.

> **Financial education is a lifelong endeavor, with each step taken enhancing the family's ability to engage in thoughtful financial planning, informed decision-making, and pursuing financial goals that align with their deepest values.**

Glossary Of Terms

Bartering: An exchange system where goods or services are directly traded for other goods or services without using money.

Budgeting: The process of creating a plan to spend your money, ensuring that you have enough funds for necessary expenses and savings goals.

Credit Card: A plastic card issued by a bank or financial institution that allows the cardholder to borrow funds with which to pay for goods and services with the promise to pay back the borrowed amount along with potential interest.

Cryptocurrency: Digital or virtual currencies that use cryptography for security and operate independently of a central bank, such as Bitcoin.

Digital Transactions: Financial transactions that occur online or through digital platforms, without the physical exchange of money.

Discretionary Spending: Non-essential expenditures that individuals have control over and can decide whether to spend based on personal preferences.

Emergency Fund: Savings account set aside to cover unexpected expenses or financial emergencies, providing a financial safety net.

Financial Literacy: The ability to understand and effectively use various financial skills, including personal financial management, budgeting, and investing.

Financial Planning Software: Computer programs that help individuals manage their finances, including budgeting, investing, and saving for retirement.

High-Yield Savings Account: A type of savings account that offers a higher interest rate compared to traditional savings accounts, allowing savers to earn more on their deposits.

Investing: The act of allocating resources, usually money, with the expectation of generating an income or profit. This can include purchasing stocks, bonds, or real estate.

Online Courses and Webinars: Educational sessions conducted over the internet that cover various topics, including financial education, allowing participants to learn remotely.

Paper Money: Currency in the form of paper notes issued by the government or central bank, representing a specific monetary value.

Savings Goals: Specific financial targets or objectives that an individual or family plans to achieve, requiring the allocation of a portion of income over time.

Seasonal Adjustments: Budget modifications made to accommodate changes in spending or income at different times of the year, such as holidays or tax season.

Stock Market: A collection of markets where stocks (pieces of ownership in businesses) are bought and sold, providing companies with access to capital in exchange for giving investors a slice of ownership.

Resources And Worksheets

Dive into the comprehensive suite of resources and worksheets included in the "Family Financial Playbook." Designed to be practical and user-friendly, these tools are your allies in navigating the financial journey ahead. From planning your family's financial future to tracking investments and setting SMART goals, everything you need to kickstart your path to financial literacy is right here.

Included Tools and Worksheets:

1. **Family Emergency Planning Checklist:** Prepare for unexpected events with a thorough checklist to safeguard your family's financial well-being.

2. **Family Financial Action Plan:** Set actionable financial goals with steps for achieving them, ensuring every family member is on the same page.

3. **Family Financial Discussion Tip Sheet:** Foster open and constructive financial conversations within your family with these helpful tips and prompts.

4. **Family Financial Playbook Goal Planner/Tracker:** Visualize and track your financial goals, making it easier to celebrate every milestone you reach together.

5. **Family Financial Tools Checklist:** Select the financial tools that best fit your family's needs with a comprehensive checklist.

6. **Family Investment Plan Worksheet:** Plan your family's investment strategy to align with your financial goals, risk tolerance, and timeline.

7. **Family Investment Tracker:** Keep a detailed log of your investments to mon-

itor performance and make informed decisions.

8. **Financial Resource Exploration Day Planner & Checklist:** Dedicate a day to exploring financial tools and resources, enhancing your family's financial literacy and management skills.

9. **Guide to Fostering Healthy Financial Discussions** Within the Family: Learn strategies for engaging in meaningful financial discussions that are educational, age-appropriate, and fun.

10. **Savings Goal Sheet:** Encourage your family, especially kids, to visualize and work towards saving for something special, tracking progress along the way.

11. **Weekly Financial Check-In Template:** Regularly review your family's financial status, including savings, spending, and progress towards goals, with this organized template.

12. **SMART Goals Worksheet:** Define and plan your financial goals using the SMART criteria, ensuring they are specific, measurable, achievable, relevant, and time-bound.

All of these can be downloaded from www.YourFamilyYourFinances.com/Playbook

Further Reading And Resources

Additional Recommended Resources:

Books:

Ramsey, D. (2013). The Total Money Makeover: A Proven Plan for Financial Fitness. Thomas Nelson. A straightforward guide for beginners on budgeting, debt reduction, and financial planning.

Sember, B. (2008). The Everything Kids' Money Book: Earn it, save it, and watch it grow! Adams Media. Introduces children to the basics of money management in an accessible way.

Bogle, J. C. (2007). The Little Book of Common Sense Investing: The Only Way to Guarantee Your Fair Share of Stock Market Returns. Wiley. Offers adults a primer on low-cost index fund investing.

Blogs:

NerdWallet (www,nerdwallet.com) : Website providing a wealth of articles on topics ranging from frugal living to retirement planning.

Podcasts:

"So Money with Farnoosh Torabi" (https://podcast.farnoosh.tv/) and "The Dave Ramsey Show" (https://www.youtube.com/@TheRamseyShowEpisodes): Podcasts offering insightful discussions, success stories, and practical tips on personal finance.

About The Author

Jeff Kikel isn't just another financial expert; he's a trailblazer, making finance fun, accessible, and utterly relatable. With over 30 years of experience, Jeff has navigated the highs and lows of personal finance, investment strategies, and family financial planning, transforming his wealth of knowledge into actionable advice for the everyday family. Jeff is a prolific author with over 10 books on Finance, Retirement, Financial Independence, and entrepreneurship.

Born with an innate curiosity about how money works and a passion for sharing knowledge, Jeff embarked on a journey that would see him wear many hats: from a financial analyst to a trusted advisor and eventually to the author and TV host beloved by families across the nation. His approach to finance is simple yet revolutionary: strip away the jargon, focus on the practical, and always keep it engaging.

Jeff's mission? To light up the path of financial literacy for families, empowering parents and kids alike to talk openly about money, set ambitious goals, and achieve financial independence. Through his engaging seminars, lively TV appearances on *Your Family*

Your Finances, and the *Family Financial Playbook*, Jeff is changing the conversation around money, one family at a time.

When he's not demystifying finance on screen or in the pages of his books, Jeff can be found running his Wealth Management Practice, Publishing Company, and Coworking Spaces. He and his wife Crystal are business partners and travel buddies who have traveled to over twenty countries.

With the *Family Financial Playbook*, Jeff invites you into a world where financial planning is not a chore, but a journey of discovery, growth, and unity. So buckle up and get ready to transform your family's financial future with Jeff Kikel as your guide—the friendliest finance guru you'll ever meet.

Keeping It Alive

Hey there! You've reached the end of "The Family Finance Playbook," and you have everything you need to master your family's finances. But you can do one more thing to make a big difference.

Leaving your honest opinion of this book on Amazon will show other families where they can find the same help you did. Your review can also help parents and teens gain the knowledge they need to feel confident about money.

I appreciate your help. Financial literacy is kept alive when we pass on our knowledge – and you're helping me to do just that.

Or Go Here:

https://www.amazon.com/review/review-your-purchases/?asin=B0DBRBF4K4

Thank Your!!!!